Who Me, Prophesy?

Dr. Jimmie Reed

PRESS

Who Me, Prophesy?
by Dr. Jimmie Reed

Printed in the United States of America

ISBN 1-594677-74-3

Most scripture quotation, unless otherwise indicated, were done in the Modern King James Version.

www.xulonpress.com

Endorsements

The prophetic movement has been spreading rapidly throughout the Body of Christ. Many who are now in the movement as well as many who are still in the seeking stage have certain legitimate questions about prophecy in their minds. If you want straightforward answers to the basic questions, look no further. Jimmie Reed, a woman of great experience and insight, gives you clear answers in this wonderful book.

C. Peter Wagner, Chancellor
Wagner Leadership Institute
Colorado Springs, Colorado

This book is a prophetic guide based on the scriptures to bring clarity to the simplest questions of the believer. Dr. Reed will launch you into the tremendous transforming power of prophecy. After reading this dynamic anointed book, yes, even you will be set free to be used by the Lord to speak the voice of God to mankind.

Pat Allen, Senior Pastor
In His Presence Worship Center
Washington, D.C.

Jimmie Reed encourages her readers by leading them through the basic beginning steps needed to understand and activate the gift of prophecy. I have traveled with Jimmie on several ministry trips and have found her prophecies both uplifting and accurate. One of her greatest abilities is teaching and equipping others to hear the voice of God, then to speak out what He is saying. She is a great encourager to the Body of Christ. I hope you will benefit from her basic one-two-three step book as you too explore the area of prophecy.

Quinn Sherrer, Author
Miracles Happen When You Pray and others
Niceville, Florida

In this era where prophecy has peaked much interest, Jimmie Reed has provided the Body of Christ with a tool that will help everyone discover their prophetic potential. In the pages of this book you will learn vital information that will be helpful for removing barriers and skepticism about prophecy. You will learn how to properly use prophecy to edify others and yourself. I highly recommend that every believer read this book!

Calvin Johnson, Senior Pastor
Solid Rock Christian Church
Colorado Springs, Colorado

Acknowledgements

My first thank you goes to an author, friend in the ministry, and mentor, Quin Sherrer, who came to me with the suggestion of this book. She gently nudged me, counseled me and believed in me to achieve this task.

I want to express my appreciation and thanks to Nancy Ruminski who was strategic in helping me to use proper wording in order to reach the reading audience we believe God would address at this time.

My children Lita, Michael, Kenneth and Jermaine as well as my spiritual parents, Earl ant Sara, have all stood by me and encouraged me in the spiritual endeavors the Lord has had for me. To each of you, I am grateful.

Bishop Bill Hamon,
President of Christian International Apostolic Network of churches and ministries, a great encourager in my life.

To my personal assistant, Robin who keeps me organized and on track.

To Ken Riggs, Glenn and Betty who have modeled a relentless pursuit of God's call which has encouraged me to keep going.

To all the intercessors that have been faithful to pray, thank you. May God Himself reward you!

Table of Contents

Foreword

by Dr. Bill Hamon

The Bible reveals that there is nothing more important for mankind than to hear the voice of God, understand clearly and respond properly. Jesus Christ is the central theme of the Bible and most important person for mankind to know. How mankind responds to the voice of God that is revealed to them though His written word, preached word and inner voice of the Holy Spirit determine their eternity. If a person does not respond to God's preached word called the gospel, he or she cannot become a child of God. God speaks to mankind through many means but most commonly through His Word. His word and will is made known primarily through the Bible. However He also uses prophecy and the illumination and conviction of the Holy Spirit.

God established two ways of making His Word known to mankind, through writing and speaking. God gave Moses His laws and words concerning the proper actions for mankind to be in proper relationship with God and one another. However, during the 1500 years of the written law of God most of the prophets of The Old Testament functioned during that time. The Written Word did not do away with the need of the word of the Lord through the prophets. God also revealed His word and will to some through dreams and visions. Likewise the New Testament Bible being written and the revealing work of the Holy Spirit did not do away with the need for ministers who are prophets and the ministry of prophesying functioning through the saints.

Jimmie Reed has made a vital contribution to the church in this book concerning saints participating in the ministry of prophesying. Some may think of prophesying as a minor issue but not the Apostle Paul, for he commanded the Corinthian Christians to "Covet to prophesy". This is the only thing that Apostle Paul told Christians to " Covet". This book gives several reasons why Christians should Covet the ministry of prophesying.

Personally I have moved in this ministry for 52 years, first as a saint in the church then in the gift-ministry of a prophet for the last 50 years. I have personally prophesied to more than 50,000 individuals from presidents of nations to small babies. More than 2000 pages of personal prophecies have been spoken to me and are recorded in five notebooks. I started training people in the prophetic through our established Schools of the Holy Spirit in 1979 I established a 300- page teaching manual for instructing and activating Christians to hear and minister the voice of the Lord. This "Manual for Ministering Spiritual Gifts" has been taught on six continents of the world training more than 210,000 Church leaders and members. I wrote a trilogy of books on Prophets, personal prophecy and the ministry of prophesying. These things are not mentioned to promote me but to assure the reader that this commendation is given with full knowledge and plenty of experience in prophetic ministry.

I can fully verify that this book presents a scriptural account of the ministry of prophesying. The principles and practices are workable and full of wisdom for a true prophetic ministry. All church ministers and members who desires to be properly used in a true prophetic ministry need to read this book.

Dr. Bill Hamon

Chairman and Founder, *Christian International Ministries Network*
Apostle over Christian International Apostolic Network
President of. CI School of Theology

Author of *The Eternal Church. Prophets and Personal Prophecy, Prophets and The Prophetic Movement, Prophets, Pitfalls and Principles, Apostles, Prophets and The Coming Moves of God,* ***The Day of the Saints***

Introduction

*Therefore my people shall know my name: therefore
they shall know in that day that I am he that doth
speak (Isaiah 52:6).*

As a young girl living in a small town in Louisiana, I had no idea God would someday use me to minister prophetically. I used to attend church only on Easter and Christmas when I got to wear a pretty lace dress and patent leather shoes. To the best of my recollection, the church I attended on those special days never mentioned the name of Jesus.

I didn't know who Jesus was during most of my formative years. I didn't understand there was a loving God Who had a divine purpose and plan for my life. I didn't know that God was personal, loving and kind, and He wanted to talk to me and know me intimately.

Even after I became a Christian at the age of 24 I still couldn't imagine all the Lord had in store for me. In all honesty, I felt behind the curve ball for many years. I didn't understand that knowing Jesus as my personal Lord and Savior was a day-by-day, step-by-step process that took time to develop. All I knew was *I just wanted to be close to Him.*

The Lord brought several people into my life who loved and discipled me. Through their consistent examples of reading the Word, praying and spending time with the Lord, these individuals showed me how to grow in intimacy with the Father. The more I followed their examples by spending time in the Word and in prayer, the more Jesus Christ unfolded Himself to me. Each day the marvels of the Bible, the love of Jesus and the richness of my Father's voice drew me deeper into a relationship with Him. It is this richness that I desire for all believers to experience in their walks with the living God. It *is my desire for you!*

After traveling throughout the world, I realize that while Christians believe in and seek God, they often lack the passion, understanding and openness to His Holy Spirit. This grieves me deeply and I believe it grieves the Father.

The scripture,

> *"My sheep hear my voice, and I know them, and they follow me"* (John 10:27),

is a beautiful illustration of how God wants us to hear His voice and to follow His instruction. Nevertheless, many Christians are taught and believe He will *only* speak through His written Word or *not at all*. This mindset is causing a large number of Christians to miss a deeper level of intimacy with God—an intimacy He is freely giving. For this reason, I believe the efforts of many Christians to emulate the life of Christ are limited to striving to love one another instead of walking in the full gifting God has given them. Why? Because *"The thief cometh but to steal, kill, and destroy"* (John 10:10). The thief's (Satan's) objective is always in opposition to the Lord. It is safe to assume that he will do everything possible to trick you into believing that you will never hear what your Father is saying. After all, why would Satan want you to seek and hear the voice of the living God?

Fortunately, you can stand in confidence against the enemy. Jesus proclaimed *"Most assuredly, I say to you, he who believes in Me, the works that I do he will do also; and **greater works than these he will do**, because I go to My Father"* (John 14:12). And the Apostle Paul declared *"I can **do all things** through Christ which strengthens me"* (Philippians 4:13). (Emphasis mine.) Doing greater works than Jesus and hearing your Heavenly Father's voice are blessings to rejoice over—*not to fe*ar. In fact, they should be a part of the average Christian's lifestyle.

Regardless of whether you speak forth the words you hear, as children of the living God you should be taught that if you seek your Father's voice He will speak back to you. By doing so, the enemy's strongholds that deafen the ears of so many Christians will be broken so the floodgates of God's abounding love will spring forth.

The King of Kings and Lord of Lords wants to commune intimately with you...*His beloved child*. Without hesitation, I believe that as you learn to hear and discern the voice of your loving Father, you will grow in confidence in Him and abound!

Dear Lord,

Walk with me as I venture into Your presence in a new and deeper way. Guide me. Show me all you have for me. Open my eyes to what your Spirit is saying. Amen.

Am I Called to Prophesy?

"Then Moses said to him, 'Are you zealous for my sake? Oh, that all the LORD'S people were prophets and that the LORD would put His Spirit upon them!'" (Numbers 11:29).

What is prophecy? Who can prophesy? How do I know if I have the gift of prophecy? These questions are often asked by those who are beginning to examine the prophetic. Each question must be answered in order to avoid confusion and fear regarding this blessing from God.

When I was a young girl, I often sensed and heard things in the Spirit realm that eventually came to pass. While I certainly didn't understand it at the time, this sensitivity was part of the gifting the Lord had placed within me even before I knew Him. Since I didn't know the prophetic existed—*let alone what it meant*—I was confused. I didn't know what to do with what I was experiencing because I had no reference point, no advisors or understanding that what I was experiencing was part of God's gifts and call on my life. If the Lord had not intervened, I would have fallen prey to the enemy's plan to destroy God's calling on my life through the fear he was trying to root within my heart.

What Is Prophecy?

The "Tyndale Bible Dictionary" defines prophecy as a group of Greek words that, in secular Greek, mean to "speak forth," "proclaim," or "announce." In biblical Greek, however, these terms always carry the connotation of "speaking, proclaiming, or announcing something under the influence of spiritual inspiration." I have come to define prophecy as many of my mentors and teachers do: "Speaking forth the mind of God under the inspiration of the Holy Spirit." It is the outflow of the heart and the very nature of God.

You probably desire to share your hopes, dreams and experiences with your children. Just like any parent, God wants to share his heart with you. King David expressed this so beautifully when he wrote:

> *"How precious also are Your thoughts to me, O God!*
> *How great is the sum of them! If I should count them,*
> *they would be more in number than the sand; When I*
> *awake, I am still with You"* (Psalms 139:17-18).

God is always thinking about His children. He wants to share His dreams, thoughts, hopes and purposes *with you*. He is a personal and intimate God Who wants you to seek Him, *yearn for Him*, and listen for Him when He speaks. I believe prophecy is vital to every Christian's walk. It is the heartbeat of the relationship between God the Father and His children.

Who Can Prophesy?

In I Corinthians 14:1-5, the Apostle Paul explained that you should yearn for spiritual gifts, *especially prophecy*. He said to pursue love, and desire spiritual gifts, especially that you may prophesy:

> *"For he who speaks in a tongue does not speak to*
> *men but to God, for no one understands him;*

however, in the spirit he speaks mysteries. But he who prophesies speaks edification and exhortation and comfort to men. He who speaks in a tongue edifies himself, but he who prophesies edifies the church. I wish you all spoke with tongues, but even more that you prophesy; for he who prophesies is greater than he who speaks with tongues, unless indeed he inter- prets, that the church may receive edification."

In the Greek, the word "edification," or oikodome, is defined as "confirmation" or "building." "Exhortation," or paraklesis, means "comfort, consolation, exhortation, entreaty" and "comfort." Paramuthia means "consolation."

According to the Apostle Paul, *"If anyone speaks, let him speak as the oracles of God. If anyone ministers, let him do it as with the ability which God supplies, that in all things God may be glorified through Jesus Christ, to whom belong the glory and the dominion forever and ever. Amen."*

"Strong's Concordance" defines the word, "oracles," (logion) as an "utterance of God." Paul is encouraging all who speak to speak the "oracles of God" by listening for His voice and then speaking forth or *prophesying* what you heard Him say.

You must intentionally seek God's voice and then speak what you hear. I believe that speaking prophetically should be a part of every believer's life. The reason I teach and activate people in the prophetic is because I desire that all of God's children learn to hear His voice. I look forward in every class I teach to the moment when a new student experiences the prophetic anointing for the first time and speaks prophetically. Every time the anointing falls, they are overcome with joy when they realize that they have truly heard the voice of the Father and spoken encouraging words to a brother or sister in Christ.

Speaking the voice of God is not only biblical, but also a bless- ing that every believer is given from the Father. Prophecy is a wonderful, intimate way in which the King of Kings and Lord of Lords communicates with each of His children. It is an anointing that everyone should desire and rejoice in.

Do I Have the Gift of Prophecy?

Many who are beginning to prophesy often ask questions, such as, "Now that I know I can hear the voice of God, does this mean that I am a prophet?" The answer is "no." It is important to understand that even though we are a prophetic people—have been given the ability to hear the voice of God—not everyone is given the gift of prophecy or called to the office of the prophet.

While some people have the gift of service and the mandate and calling that goes with it, everyone in the Body of Christ is called to serve. The prophetic operates in the same way. While there are some people called to the office of the prophet and have the mandate that goes with it, all Christians can *hear* the voice of God and prophesy for the exhortation, edification and comfort of the Church.

The Prophetic Anointing

As I have said, all of God's children can hear His voice, and therefore, *can* prophesy. However, it is important to understand that the vast majority of believer's will prophesy in the first and most basic level—the "prophetic anointing." At this level, the Holy Spirit touches an individual and the believer speaks what he has heard. This type of prophecy is often seen in Charismatic churches and circles, and is used to inspire and encourage. The Apostle Paul was referring to this type of prophecy when he said it was his desire that all would prophesy. This level of prophecy is non-correctional and non-directional, and its purpose is to build up and to comfort the Church.

The prophetic anointing has been activated time and time again in my ministry. Often those who are new to the prophetic will attend a class and after some basic instruction, are soon hearing the voice of God and speaking forth words of edification and comfort. This prophetic edification can be life changing. I have seen the Holy Spirit move mightily through this anointing. For this reason, we need to take prophetic words from individuals who prophesy at this level seriously by pondering and evaluating them through prayer and time with the Lord. Remember, *the anointing is from the*

Holy Spirit. Therefore, the word can powerfully affect the lives of those who receive it. It should not be discarded simply because the deliverer of the message is young, inexperienced or not considered to be a prophet.

The Gift of Prophecy

Individuals with the gift of prophecy regularly experience revelation from the Lord. This revelation can come in many different forms, including impressions, visions, unction's of God, dreams and words of knowledge (these will be defined in a later chapter).

The gift of prophecy is a sovereign endowment birthed within the believer by the Holy Spirit. It is a gift of the Spirit written about in I Corinthians 12:10-11 that says, *"To another the working of miracles, to another prophecy, to another discerning of spirits, to another, different kinds of tongues, to another the interpretation of tongues. But one and the same Spirit works all these things, distributing to each one individually as He wills. It is wholly and fully irrevocable."*

While the gifting at this level is of the Spirit, it must be matured by and tempered with wisdom as it is developed and grown. Just as any young pastor must grow and develop in their gift of teaching, a person with the gift of prophecy must also grow. After all, gifts of the Spirit are not based on one's maturity but are given as the Spirit wills. It is important for grace and patience to be extended to those who are growing in their prophetic gifting.

Just as God blesses individuals with musical talent, or the ability to play the piano or another instrument at will, the gift of prophecy is given as the Spirit wills. It is not dependent upon a special prophetic anointing from the Holy Spirit but is a clearly defined, God given ability that can and should be used and exercised on a regular basis for the exhortation, edification and comfort of the Church. The Apostle Paul wrote,

"Having then gifts differing according to the grace

that is given to us, whether prophecy, let us prophesy according to the proportion of faith."

We need to look at the gift of prophecy as a wonderful blessing from God for those who have the gift and for the Body of Christ. We need to encourage those with this gift to use it within the boundaries and guidelines given in Scripture. Those who have received the gift of prophecy should step out according to their measure of faith and work to mature in this gift so they can continue to uphold and encourage the Bride of Christ.

Prophetic Ministers

Those whose gift of prophecy has been developed, tested and recognized are often placed within churches and ministries as prophetic ministers. Because of education, development and experience, their gift has matured, and thus, been elevated to a higher level. At this level of the prophetic, wisdom, maturity and the Holy Spirit come together to build a broader scope of prophecy. While the focus remains along the lines of I Corinthians 14:3, there may be times when the Lord opens the door to new revelation, and sometimes, correction.

The gifting at this level is the same gifting given by the Holy Spirit in the previous level except that it has been developed, which significantly increases the person's ability to discern the voice of God versus the voice of the enemy or his flesh.

Graham Cooke discusses this in his book, *"Developing Your Prophetic Gifting."* He says,

"People need training in prophecy as much as they do in prayer, warfare, worship, sharing their faith and praying for the sick...As we receive training, discipleship and opportunity to move in the gift, we develop our listening potential. We learn to filter out our own thoughts, discern the voice of the enemy and hold on to the word of the Lord. In prophetic

ministry there is less mixture; we are growing into the gift and establishing credibility and good track records."

Prophetic ministers have often paid a price for their development. As a result, they have not only grown in their abilities to prophesy, but have also grown in character, wisdom and their personal relationships with the Lord.

The Office of the Prophet

The office of the prophet is a very specific gift. It falls under the fivefold ministry calling found in Ephesians 4:11-12:

"And He Himself gave some to be apostles, some prophets, some evangelists, and some pastors and teachers, for the equipping of the saints for the work of ministry, for the edifying of the body of Christ." Internationally renowned prophet, author and head of Christian International Ministries, Dr. Bill Hamon, explains the fivefold ministry gifting in his book *"Prophets and Personal Prophecy."* He says, *"This gifting was not an external endowment like a birthday present. Instead, it was an investment of Christ's mantle for one of the five ministries of Jesus–a divine impartation of Christ's own nature, wisdom, and power for each particular kind of performance. All five, when moving in full maturity, represent Christ's full ministry to the Church. These ministries are not just an extension of the Body ministry, but an extension of the headship of Christ to His Body, the Church."*

This means that the office of the prophet was designed with a mandate or an authorization from God for the equipping of believers for ministry. This gift functions at a higher level of ministry than the gift of prophecy. At this level, the prophet is activated in all of the functions that are seen in both Old and New Testaments.

Those who occupy the office of the prophet have a heightened need of credibility, which usually has been established over time. Although the prophecies given by the person who holds this office are nearly 100 percent accurate, he is not infallible. However, his experience, knowledge, wisdom and ability to hear the voice of the Father should be respected and heeded.

Those who occupy the office of the prophet flow not only in exhortation, edification and comfort, but also in areas of instruction, rebuke, revelation and guidance. In other words, they speak forth whatever the Lord desires to speak for the continued sanctification and perfecting of His Church.

The office of the prophet is not to be taken lightly. It is a governmental mantle given by Christ Himself. Therefore, godly wisdom *must be present* in the lives of all who are given this title. This gifting is amazing and costly. As brothers and sisters in Christ we should pray for those who stand in this office just as we do for the other great men and women of God who are gifted in other areas.

Regardless of where God has placed you in the prophetic spectrum, once activated, this blessing will bring hope, greater intimacy with God and revival deep within your soul. Recently I had the pleasure of seeing the fruit of the prophetic anointing activated in the life of one of my close friends. Renee, a dedicated and gifted intercessor says,

> *"I have been saved for many years and no church ever introduced this gift to me as it was presented during these prophetic classes. They gave me a greater understanding of the prophetic, and now I can help other people hear the voice of God. They need to know God loves them enough to speak to them."*

Because of a growing understanding of the prophetic, Renee was inspired to share with and reach out to those she interceded for at a new level. The more she ministered, the more people's lives were changed. Renee personally found a greater intimacy with the

Father which she had not experienced before. Now she is motivated to go and share this intimacy with others. This is a beautiful example of how prophecy, when properly defined, brings healing.

Father, I thank You and praise You that it is Your heart's desire to speak to me and through me. It is a blessing to know and serve a God Who is intimately involved with every aspect of my life. Father, in the name of Jesus I ask that You will grow my ability to hear Your voice. Holy Spirit, I ask that You will come with Your anointing and help me to minister as You desire when You desire. If You have blessed me with the gift of prophecy, I ask that this gift would be grown and matured in my life so that I might produce great fruit for Your kingdom. Thy will be done in and through me, Father. Amen.

Questions:
1. What is prophecy?
2. How does I Corinthians 14:1 say you should seek to prophesy?
3. What is God's purpose for prophecy?
4. As a child of God, can you prophesy?
5. What are the various levels of prophecy?

Exposing the Lies of the Enemy

*"Lead me in Your truth and teach me, For You are
the God of my salvation;
On You I wait all the day" (Psalms 25:5).*

"Isn't it true that if a prophetic word you get doesn't come to pass, it was false?" a lady by the name of Peggy asked at a conference recently. I realized that she had fallen into one of the most common traps of the enemy regarding prophecy. She believed the lie that if a prophetic word does not come to pass then it is false.

In response to her question I asked, "What if there had been numerous prophecies over your pastor in his youth that he would become a pastor? Yet, he never took time to study the Word of God, spend time in God's presence and took no courses to lead him to that destiny. Do you think he would be your pastor today?" She quickly answered by saying, "Well, no, he wouldn't be my pastor."

I then began to share how God often speaks to us through His Holy Scriptures about the path He has designed for us. Yet, because we choose to not act upon what He has spoken, His rhema Word doesn't come to pass. I Corinthians 1:9 says,

> *"God is faithful, by whom you were called into the
> fellowship of His Son, Jesus Christ our Lord."* God
> is trustworthy and true to His promises.

You *can* depend on Him. Yet, some people who receive a prophetic word are undependable and fail to move toward their calling. If you do not move in the direction the Lord communicates through a prophetic word, it does not mean the word was false. Perhaps you were unwilling to be intentional in the areas in which the Lord asked you. He will not *make* you move into the destiny He has planned for you any more than He made you receive salvation. You must decide to respond to His leading.

A biblical example related to this lie of the enemy is found in Jonah. After the fish spat Jonah out on dry land, the Bible says,

> *"So Jonah arose and went to Nineveh, according to the word of the Lord. Now Nineveh was an exceedingly great city, a three-day journey in extent. And Jonah began to enter the city on the first day's walk. Then he cried out and said, 'Yet forty days, and Nineveh shall be overthrown!'"* (Jonah 3:3-4).

Although Jonah's prophecy was accurate, the people of Nineveh confessed their sin and invoked God's mercy. God repented of His anger toward the people of Nineveh and the destruction prophesied by Jonah did not come to pass.

Was Jonah a false prophet because his word did not come true? No. Was the prophetic word he spoke accurate although it did not come to pass? Yes, because the end result had nothing to do with the validity of Jonah's prophecy. Jonah 3:10 says, *"Then God saw their works, that they turned from their evil way; and God relented from the disaster that He had said He would bring upon them, and He did not do it."*

This verse clearly demonstrates that the change in the hearts of the people of Nineveh caused God's mercy to overcome His impending judgment. It was God's decision to repent of His anger, however, in doing this He did not render Jonah's prophecy false. Rather, the prophecy was so undeniably true that it turned the hearts of a nation and saved them from certain destruction.

Christians need to be careful about discarding God's Word. If the Word you receive lines up with Scripture, you need to pray over it and ask God how He wants you to act upon it. You should then seek God's heart and be willing to move with purpose toward His direction and call.

Strive for the Fruit of the Spirit

Many Christian believe that the Fruit of the Spirit is the primary indication of God working in their lives. While I would never argue that the fruit of the Spirit (love, joy, peace, longsuffering, gentleness, goodness, faith, meekness, and temperance) must be evident in the life of every believer, a life without the gifts of the Spirit is contrary to God's plan as well.

Fruit is grown, not given. Good soil fertilized with godly character is established as you begin to walk in freedom and use the spiritual gifts God has blessed you with. This makes way for the abounding growth of the sweet fruit of the Spirit.

The Apostle Paul understood the necessity of spiritual gifts and encouraged believers to seek and develop them. He acknowledged the need for spiritual gifts as a key to fruitfulness when he said,

> *"I thank my God always on your behalf, for the grace of God which is given you by Jesus Christ; That in every thing ye are enriched by him, in all utterance, and in all knowledge; Even as the testimony of Christ was confirmed in you: So that ye come behind in no gift; waiting for the coming of our Lord Jesus Christ"* (I Corinthians 1:4-7).

Spiritual gifts brought depth to Paul's ministry and he praised those who walked in them. As you learn to walk in the Spirit and mature in spiritual gifts, the anointing that comes with the gifts will grow and develop. You will be strengthened through time in prayer, the Word and exercising your gifts. You will then be less likely to fall into fleshly things that occur apart from the fruit of the Spirit. Paul spoke of this maturing process in Hebrews 5:14 when he said,

*"But solid food belongs to those who are of full age,
that is, those who by reason of use have their senses
exercised to discern both good and evil."*

When you begin to understand that spiritual gifts are empowerments provided by God to manifest His Kingdom, your attitude toward them will change. I pray that all believers will experience the freedom with the Lord to examine the gifts of the Spirit. As that happens, the fruit of the Spirit should become more and more evident.

While I believe in the gifts of the Spirit, I also believe that the use of the gifts without the steady development of godly character has been a mistake made by many in the Body of Christ. This error has caused those who have been open to the gifts to reject prophecy, which is contrary to Scripture (1 Thessalonians 5:20-21).

Chuck Pierce addresses this issue in his book titled *"When God Speaks"*:

*"When something is in the beginning stages there is
often a lack of maturity and a lack of understanding,
which can open the door to flakiness. When flakiness
springs up, there is a tendency to say that something
(in this case prophecy) is more trouble than it's
worth. But Paul says no. Don't shut it down. Don't
quench the Spirit. Let it happen, test everything and
hold on to what is good."*

In light of this statement, we should take note of those who are pursuing spiritual gifts but not cultivating spiritual fruit. Godly correction should be given when necessary. I say this with caution, however. As a Body, we have historically punished those who have sought the gifts and have wounded many of God's children, which ultimately has contributed to a backlash against godly discipline within the Church. For this reason, I believe we *must* become more balanced in our pursuit of correcting errors. We must seek restoration for those who have fallen in their zeal due to a lack of character. We must make certain that we do not appear to rule out and dismiss the gifts while correcting the believer who is pursuing spiritual gifts without godly character. We need balance and love that can only come from the seeking the Lord Jesus Christ.

The Gifts Are Only for the Chosen Few

Many people believe only certain individuals are called to ministry. These individuals are mentored and groomed to fit the mold the leadership desires, and are soon placed in high-ranking positions within the church or organization in which they were developed.

I would never disagree that there are individuals who are called to work in the Church whose gifts need to be developed. However, statistics show that roughly two percent of the Body does the work within the Church, which means 98 percent ministers outside of the Church. Shouldn't this group of people also be equipped to minister and fulfill the great commission? When you examine who Jesus called to follow Him, you will find that from fishermen to tax collectors, the Lord looked at the hearts of His disciples, not individuals who fit a certain mold. The Bible admonishes parents to teach their children the Word and to help develop their spiritual gifts. Jesus proclaimed,

> *"Let the little children come to Me, and do not forbid them; for of such is the kingdom of heaven"* (Matthew 19:14).

The Lord did not withhold Himself or His blessing from the young—nor *should we*. Brandice, a young lady who attends our church, says:

> *"For years I was taught that there were only a few who were called to ministry, and within a church setting, children should only be seen and not heard. Because of this, I believed prophecy and the other gifts were only for adults and specifically for adults*

in positions of authority within a church setting. When I began to attend Christian International of the Rockies, I soon found that the gifts of the Spirit, including prophecy, were not withheld from me. In fact, I was encouraged to participate in classes that helped me to grow in my personal relationship with Jesus Christ, as well as my gifting. Now I am able to minister to people who I never dreamed I would because I am operating within the gifting and under the anointing the Lord has given me."

It has been my pleasure to watch Brandice grow and develop into a young lady with great prophetic gifting. I have rejoiced as the Lord has solidified His calling and purpose in her life. I have also been blessed through strong words of edification and exhortation the Lord has spoken to me through her. The gifts of the Spirit have blossomed and grown in a magnificent way in Brandice's life. His hand upon her is an example to us all.

We Should Only Seek Jesus

One day I was talking with a young man named Ted, who was raised in a strict Evangelical setting. As we spoke, I realized he believed we should not desire the gifts, but that our only focus should be on our personal relationship with the Lord. While I agree that God should be our main passion—our first love, the Bible is abundantly clear that the pursuit of the gifts follows that passion to bring us to full maturity in Christ.

To fully expose this lie of the enemy we must again examine I Corinthians 14:1, which admonishes us to *"Follow after charity, and desire spiritual gifts."* The Greek word for "desire," zeloo, means to covet earnestly. Another definition means "to have great desire for, to be jealous over and to be zealously affected." It is taken from the Greek root word, "zelos," which means "fervency of mind or an emotional jealousy. It also means to "have a tremendous passionate zeal, a burning and yearning to be used, and an intense hunger to see something happen." It is God's desire for us to seek out, to yearn for and intensely desire His gifts.

Jack Deere, a strong man of God who taught at Dallas Theological Seminary for many years, has written several books about his transforming experience by the Holy Spirit. In his book *"Surprised by the Power of the Spirit,"* he says,

> *"As soon as I was convinced that the Scriptures taught the gifts of the Spirit are for today, I began to pursue them diligently. The most important things I have done in pursuing the gifts has been to pray very specifically for the gifts I felt the Lord wanted to give me. Even though the Holy Spirit distributes the gifts to each one just as he wills, (I Cor. 12:11), Paul still encouraged the Corinthians to pray for gifts…God could also make you a great Bible scholar if he wanted to, but I don't know any great Bible scholars who got that way without diligently pursuing the knowledge of the Bible. Nor do I know any great evangelists who go that way without diligently pursuing evangelism."*

I agree with Jack. Believers need to diligently pursue the gifts and ask God for the fullness of all He has for them. For example, what if your father worked hard all of his life and arranged to leave a good deal of his estate to you when he died? But instead of waiting until his death, he chose to give it to you early because he knew it would benefit you and your family. However, you chose not to receive the wealth yet because you wanted to spend time getting to know him more. Do you think your father would appreciate that sentiment more than you loving him enough to enjoy the gift he had worked hard to give you? I believe our heavenly Father feels the same way. He first wants a relationship in which you grow, develop and know the sound of His voice. He also desires to fill you with His Spirit and bless you with spiritual gifts so you can benefit and minister to those around you.

Those Who Want the Gifts of the Spirit Are Egotistical and Strive for Selfish Gain

Some people with questionable motives have sought spiritual gifts. As a result, a negative light has been cast in some circles on those who desire the gifts. Paul addresses this issue in Philippians 1:15-18 when he says:

> *"Some indeed preach Christ even from envy and strife, and some also from goodwill: The former preach Christ from selfish ambition, not sincerely, supposing to add affliction to my chains; but the latter out of love, knowing that I am appointed for the defense of the gospel. What then? Only that in every way, whether in pretense or in truth, Christ is preached; and in this I rejoice, yes, and will rejoice."*

The Apostle Paul's attitude is an example for us to follow. We must keep our hearts focused on the paramount purpose of spiritual gifts, which is the furthering of the kingdom and the preaching of the gospel. When we take our eyes off of ourselves and work to emulate the servant life of Christ, it is more difficult to become wrapped up in our own needs, wants and desires. However, our flesh is weak and we should be willing to humble ourselves and regularly cry out: *"Create in me a clean heart, O God, And renew a steadfast spirit within me"* (Psalms 51:10). When we operate within our gifting with a humble and contrite heart, we can then fulfill the purpose for our gifts—to minister to others.

In his book, *The Holy Spirit Activating God's Power in Your Life*, the Rev. Billy Graham says:

> *"Whether the Holy Spirit gives us one or several, it is important for us to do two things: First we should recognize the gift or gifts God has given us. Second, we should nurture those gifts and do everything, humanly speaking, to improve them as we use them. One who has the gift of prophecy should be better*

able to fill this role with the passage of every year of his life. And the person with the gift of wisdom should be wiser at the end than he was at the beginning."

Prophecy Leads You into the Hands of the Demonic

As I have traveled to minister, teach and train others to desire to prophesy, I have learned that some believers think pursuing the prophetic anointing "opens you up to the demonic." I am happy to inform them that the Bible is ordained and inspired by God. Knowing this, they can be sure that the Holy Spirit would not have inspired the apostles to write about pursuing gifts, especially prophecy, if they were demonic. The psalmist proclaimed:

"For the LORD God is a sun and shield; The LORD will give grace and glory; No good thing will He withhold from those who walk uprightly" (Psalms 84:11).

God will not allow the enemy to overcome and defeat those who are seeking the gifts He ordained for His Bride. It is important to note that the devil will oppose everyone who desires to grow in the Word. Paul says

"For though we walk in the flesh, we do not war according to the flesh. For the weapons of our warfare are not carnal but mighty in God for pulling down strongholds"

(II Corinthians 10:3-4). As you enter into a deeper relationship with the Lord, the devil will try to establish strongholds in your life to discourage you. Do not be discouraged because as Paul wrote in II Corinthians, God has given you spiritual weapons to defeat spiritual forces. As you seek God, you can rest knowing that He will be your shield and provide you with the strategy to war against the enemy when he attacks.

The victory over the devil and his cohorts has already been won. Therefore, you can embrace prophecy because God will not disappoint you. Deuteronomy 31:8 says, *"And the LORD, He is the One who goes before you. He will be with you; He will not leave you nor forsake you; do not fear nor be dismayed."* Our heavenly Father has the answers. He holds the keys. You need to desire the gifts, and know that when you experience spiritual opposition that He will never fail you or forsake you.

Loving Father,

Thank You that You desire to speak to me and through me. Forgive me for believing the lies of the enemy. I ask You to break down any strongholds and biases these lies may have rooted within me. I want the freedom to hear Your voice and speak forth what I have heard as You desire and direct. Thank You Father for being bigger, stronger and more powerful than any lie of the enemy. I praise You for Your freedom and now ask You to help me to grow in my ability to hear Your voice. Thank You, Father. Amen.

Questions:
1. Have you believed any of these lies about prophecy and the prophetic gift?
2. Has this chapter helped you to overcome these lies? If so, how?
3. Was Jonah a false prophet?
4. Is fruit given or grown?

Overcoming Fear through Faith and Perfect Love

"The fear of man brings a snare, but whoever trusts in the Lord shall be safe" Proverbs 29:25 (NKJV).

Have you ever felt compelled to ask someone if you can pray for them, and then your mind was flooded with thoughts, such as, "I'm sure they're fine. I'm just imagining that. I'd be crazy to ask them. I'd look like a fool." And unfortunately the urgency to pray left as quickly as the initial thought to pray?

Sadly, when God is prompting us to pray for someone, we oftentimes mistake these thoughts as our own. I believe, however, these thoughts are often *prophetic thoughts* from the Holy Spirit, which if acted upon could bring healing and restoration to that individual. But because of fear and insecurity, healing, restoration or revelation is not given to the person to whom the Lord is directing us.

Fear is not of God. Second Timothy 1:7 says,

"For God has not given us a spirit of fear, but of power and of love and of a sound mind."

I have watched again and again as God's people have missed opportunities to minister to one another. Even worse, some have missed their callings as a direct result of the bondage of fear. Overcoming fear is crucial for anyone who desires to walk in intimacy with the Lord. Dr. Creflo A. Dollar, author and pastor of World Changers Church International, describes in his book, *"Uprooting the Spirit of Fear,"* how the Holy Spirit brings an anointing of blessing in the believer's life, while the spirit of fear brings a curse.

> *"When a believer is influenced by the Holy Spirit, we call it an anointing. This anointing of the Holy Spirit empowers and emboldens ('gives courage to,' or 'causes to be bold'). His empowerment enables a Christian to do things they could never do in their own strength and wisdom. In a sense, the presence of a spirit of fear in your life also brings with it—a negative, destructive force that keeps us from fulfilling what God desires. Instead of empowering you, fear paralyzes you. Instead of giving you wisdom, fear causes you to make poor decisions. Instead of the blessing of the true anointing of the Holy Spirit, the demonic anointing of a spirit of fear brings a curse."*

I agree with Dr. Dollar. I have seen the bondage the spirit of fear brings in the lives of so many precious believers. For example, there was a woman who was controlled and bound by fear at a recent conference where I taught on the prophetic. While those around her began to step into the prophetic anointing and speak prophetic words of encouragement, she could barely utter a sound. Tears soon welled up in her eyes and the enemy pounded her with feelings of inadequacy and failure. Recognizing that fear was overcoming her, many in the class began to minister the truth of the Lord's heart and love *for her* through prophetic words. Slowly, the bondage of fear began to loosen its grip as she experienced the love of the Lord. However, because fear had taken root in her life, she was unable to fully experience the prophetic anointing or the joy of speaking forth words of exhortation and comfort to those around her. Sadly, I have seen instances like this time and time again.

Fear is one of the most powerful tools the enemy uses against God's people. It prevents them from moving into a deeper relationship with the Father and into the fullness of the gifts. The parable of the talents in Matthew 25:14-30 illustrates how the Lord deals with those ruled by fear. Fear cannot be your master if you are to move forward and prosper spiritually. When the man who had been given one talent hid it because he was afraid to invest it, his master responded by saying,

> *"You wicked and lazy servant, you knew that I reap where I have not sown, and gather where I have not scattered seed. So you ought to have deposited my money with the bankers, and at my coming I would have received back my own with interest. So take the talent from him, and give it to him who has ten talents. For to everyone who has, more will be given, and he will have abundance; but from him who does not have, even what he has will be taken away. And cast the unprofitable servant into the outer darkness. There will be weeping and gnashing of teeth."*

The lesson of the parable of the talents is obvious. The Lord does not want you to hide your gifts because you are afraid to use them. He wants you to use your gifts wisely for the growth of His Church. Fear causes you to focus on yourself, while spiritual gifts compel you to minister to those around you.

Fear *is a sin*. Romans 14:23 says,

> *"But he who doubts is condemned if he eats, because his eating is not from faith; But he who doubts is condemned if he eats, because he does not eat from faith; for whatever is not from faith is sin."*

You sin against God when you allow fear to restrict and bind you. How should you walk toward the Lord? The answer is simple: *by faith*. Hebrews 11:1 says,

"Faith is the substance of things hoped for, the evidence of things not seen."

Saint Augustine once said, "Faith is believing what one cannot see, and the reward for faith is to see what one believes."

The Bible is filled with examples of people who have walked by faith. When Abraham was told to sacrifice his only son Isaac, he obeyed believing that God would provide a ram for the sacrifice in place of his son. Moses lifted his staff above the Red Sea believing that the Lord would part it. By faith he obeyed God, knowing that He would save the Israelites from the Egyptian army that was pursuing them. David battled the giant Goliath, proclaiming, *"This day the Lord will deliver you into my hand,"* although the only thing he had in his hand was a few smooth stones and a sling shot. Esther revealed to the king that she was a Jew, believing God would not only protect her, but her nation as well.

The common thread to all of these stories is that each person had to first walk by faith and take action in faith before the Lord released His truth, blessing and restoration. You can deduce, therefore, that walking by faith means to obey God's command as an act of your will, believing that His purpose and plan for your life will prevail. Walking by faith releases blessings, sets the captives free, strengthens and uplifts you, pulls down strongholds, destroys yokes, and pleases God. Although it may not feel like it at the time, stepping out in faith is a *place of safety.* As a prophetic people, you must be willing to step out in faith as the Holy Spirit leads you. Walking in faith overcomes the spirit of fear and allows you to step into the rich blessing of the peace that transcends human understanding!

Remember Hebrews 11:6, which says:

"But without faith it is impossible to please Him, for he who comes to God must believe that He is, and that He is a rewarder of those who diligently seek Him" (NKJV).

Examine your heart. Are there areas where you have been in bondage to the spirit of fear? Are there areas where the Lord is calling you to step out in faith, yet you're too afraid of how you might look or what people might say? Ask the Holy Spirit to identify strongholds of fear in your life. Take a moment now and pray the following prayer,

> *"Lord, thank You for being a God Who is not One of fear but rather One of power and love. Thank You for dying on the Cross for me so I don't have to be in bondage to fear. I praise You and ask You to forgive me for the areas in my life where I have given into fear (fear of man, fear of failure, fear of public humiliation, fear of exposure, fear of making a mistake, fear of being wrong, fear of retribution or any other areas that have come to mind). In the name of the Lord Jesus Christ, I break all agreements with the spirit of fear. I ask the Holy Spirit to come into those areas of my life and fill me with godly boldness and faith. Father, I want to serve You in wisdom and truth. I want to please You throughout my life as I step out in faith. Please break the yoke of fear that I have carried and replace it with Your mantle of faith and love. I pray all of these things in the mighty Name of the Lord Jesus Christ. Amen."*

Now, step out in faith! Grab hold of the talents the Lord has given you and begin to obey for His loving voice. The next time you sense the Lord asking you to pray for someone, be bold and allow the Holy Spirit to lead you. *Take action! W*alk in the leading of the Spirit and see your fruit grow!

Breaking the Spirit of Fear in the Body Through God's Love

Overcoming fear and walking by faith is important to every member in the Body of Christ. As individuals we can make choices and ask the Holy Spirit to fill us with His boldness. As a Body, the issue is far more complex. For centuries, the enemy has worked hard to establish long-running divisions between believers through disagreement on doctrinal issues. These divisions have resulted in a climate of discord. In light of this friction within the Body, it is difficult for many to step out in faith to use their gifts because they fear a backlash from those they love if they venture out of their spiritual comfort zones. However, the Body of Christ must first be an expression of the Father's love before it can step out in faith as a unified force. First John 4:18 says,

> *"There is no fear in love; but perfect love casts out fear, because fear involves torment."* (Emphasis mine.)

As I previously stated, fear is not of God. The Body of Christ therefore must embrace the love of the Father and create loving, safe environments where teaching, encouragement and protection from undue criticism will become the norm. The objective for believers is to reach for the high calling Paul explains in Hebrews 12:28:

> *"Therefore, since we are receiving a kingdom which cannot be shaken, let us have grace, by which we may serve God acceptably with reverence and godly fear."*

Amy Carmichael once said, "Thank God he doesn't measure grace out in teaspoons." Oh, how I agree! For it will be the grace of the Father and His abounding love that creates safe, compassionate environments throughout the Body of Christ so that each individual believer can move within different doctrinal settings without condemnation or fear.

I believe that as the Body assumes a posture of love, understanding and patience, it will enable believers to step out in faith and speak the heart and mind of the Father. This vital expression of God's love will help release those in the bondage of fear. According to Romans 8:37: *"We are more than conquerors through Him who loved us."* This means the spirit of fear can and will be conquered by and through God's love! What a privilege and joy it is for me to see fear defeated in God's children on a regular basis.

Robin, a worship leader who attended one of our prophetic classes, says,

> *"Taking this class helped give me more confidence to share some of the things I sensed the Lord was telling me. Now in worship I am more confident that I can hear from a loving God. Before I heard wonderful words in song—blessings from the Father—but I didn't know what to do with them. Now, with a release from my pastor, God has been using me to minister in song."*

Mary, who attended the same class, said,

> *"I felt real timid before taking this class. The Holy Spirit would reveal things for me to give to others and I would be doubting and stalling. This class helped me to learn to release the words without fear."*

Your faith grows as you learn to come against the spirit of fear. Once fear is overcome and defeated, you can more easily move with confidence into the faith of things not yet seen and share what the Lord is telling you! Praise the Lord! You need not fear. You just need faith in your loving Father, knowing that He will guide and keep you safe as you walk in the Spirit.

"Dear Lord Jesus, I praise You that Your Word says that Perfect Love casts out all fear. I praise You that You are Perfect Love. As I learn to walk in Your love, freedom from fear and anxiety will come! Father, in the Name of Jesus, I bind fear away from me and I choose to walk in Your love and acceptance, not only for me, but also for others. Thank You, my Lord and King, for loving me so much that You talk to me and sing songs over me (Zephaniah 3:17). Amen"

Questions:
1. Why does the enemy work so hard to instill fear into those who serve the Lord?
2. What are some instances in which you were afraid to obey God's leading?
3. How would you handle the situation after reading this chapter?
4. Is there a verse in this chapter or the Bible that can help you overcome fear? Memorize it so that it can help you the next time you encounter fear.

Can I Really Hear God's Voice?

"For prophecy never came by the will of man, but holy men of God spoke as they were moved by the Holy Spirit" (II Peter 1:21).

My son Kenneth once sang in an all-state choir in Colorado. He was one of two youth picked from his school to sing in a choir with hundreds of other students. I could distinguish his tenor voice clearly in the midst of all the other voices. Even when I wasn't trying to zone in on his voice, I could hear him clearly. Why? Because I have grown to know my son's voice over the years. It is imprinted on my heart and in my mind. I am able to single out his voice from all others.

The same is true with your heavenly Father. Jesus explained this principle in John 10:

> *"After he has gathered his own flock, he walks ahead of them, and they follow him because they recognize his voice. They won't follow a stranger; they will run from him because they don't recognize his voice."*

Discerning, or listening for the voice of the Lord is part of the growth process that all believers should experience. Hearing God's voice is not hard, but each individual must *continually exercise* his or her spiritual senses in order to increase their "receptive" abilities. Chuck Pierce addresses this issue in his book, *When God Speaks:*

> *"Hearing the voice of God is not as difficult as some might think. I have found that many of God's people are hearing Him, but have not perceived that it is His voice. To perceive means to take hold of, feel, comprehend, grasp mentally, recognize, observe, or become aware of something by discerning. We must learn to perceive God's voice, which will help us understand His will for our lives."*

To perceive the voice of God, it is important to grasp the reality that He speaks to His children in many ways—through His word, impressions, visions, dreams, and words of knowledge. He speaks through the Holy Spirit to your human spirit (I Thessalonians 5:23) to bring direction and guidance. Truly, there are no limits on how God communicates His love and plan to His children.

God Speaks through His Word

God's Word is a prophetic love song to His children. There are words of caution, direction and even reprimand, but anyone who reads the Bible cannot deny the Lord's love that springs forth from each book and chapter. Regardless of your circumstances, the Bible holds the keys to truth regarding your particular struggle. Begin to look at the Word of God as His personal love song to you. When you view Scripture in this manner, it will draw you to Him, allowing His truth and light to illuminate the dark areas deep within.

Mary Geegh, a missionary to India for 38 years, talks about the Word of God speaking into the circumstances of a believer. In the book, *God Guides,* she writes,

> *"A teacher in another elementary school was very unhappy; deeply distressed over something she*

could not share. She learned to 'be still' and 'listen' to God for His guidance. Then one day she was meditating on the Lord's Prayer. Two words struck her with great illumination: 'Our Father.' Then she told us her story. She was born to her mother out of wedlock. Her mother gave her to the Christian nurse who attended her. This nurse was not married and had a home, so she took the child and brought her up as her own child. All of us who knew this teacher thought she was the daughter of this Christian nurse. The teacher said, 'Only today I realized that I have a father! Our Father in Heaven! How thankful I am that He chose me to be His daughter!' From that day her life was radiant...From then on Pamma was a great Christian teacher."

Isn't God's Word amazing? Two words illuminated by the Holy Spirit brought deep healing to replace the hurt carried in that teacher's life. You must never dismiss the power of Scripture because God has given them to guide, direct and heal. Discerning or hearing the voice of God should be rooted deeply and soundly in Scripture. If not, it will be easy for believers to get off base and enter into a spirit of error.

Impressions

Spiritual impressions are one way God communicates with the Body of Christ that is overlooked by believers because they tend to attribute them to personal intuition and discernment. For example, I had a strong impression one morning during my devotions that a key individual was not going to be able to travel with me on an upcoming ministry trip. It seemed unlikely to my natural way of thinking for this person to back out at the last minute. "She is my good friend who has always been reliable," I thought. I have learned over the years, however, to not take impressions like this lightly, so I took a moment to consider before the Lord whether what I was hearing was from Him.

In all honestly, as I pondered what I was sensing, nothing in the natural added up. Everything for the trip seemed to be in place. Every piece of information I had, including a conversation with this individual the night before which indicated she would be traveling with me. Reality, however, is often different from the way things appear. Knowing this, the Lord will, at times, give us a "heads up" to prepare us for the unexpected and I believe this is exactly what was happening in the case of my ministry trip.

The impression continued to surface throughout the day. Though I hate to admit it, instead of praying over it more, I continued to push it away so I could focus on what I needed to accomplish. However, the Lord would not relent. The impression kept coming. I went to bed that night wondering if the impression might be the enemy trying to bring disruption, or was it the Lord trying to show me that things were about to change.

I received a phone call from the woman soon after I arrived at my office the next morning. She had had an unexpected death in her family and would be able to go for only part of the trip. It was clear to me then that the Lord, in His mercy, had been speaking through that "nagging" impression to help prepare me for this news. Out of His abounding love, He opened the door for another individual to travel with me so I was not without support on my ministry trip.

Impressions can be likened to "whispers from the Lord" to the very depths of our souls. It is important to not downplay or minimize this form of communication because though easy to miss or dismiss, it is a prophetic tool God uses to bring healing and restoration.

Audible Voice or Internal Voice

First Samuel 3 is one of my favorite Bible stories. I love it because the Lord spoke to Samuel without overwhelming him. He did not use a booming voice that caused Samuel to tremble with fear. He used a soft voice that sounded much like Eli, his master, and in doing so, the Lord trained Samuel how to hear and know His voice.

As you read the story of Samuel you see that because the Lord's voice was unfamiliar to him, when Samuel heard the Lord calling his name he rushed to Eli's bedside to ask what he needed. Eli recognized the voice Samuel was hearing was the voice of the Lord and he instructed Samuel that when the voice spoke again, to say, *"Speak Lord, for your servant hears"* (1 Samuel 3:9, NKJ). Samuel followed Eli's instructions and heard all the Lord had to say to him. A mere child hearing the audible voice of God—what a marvel! As a result of his obedience, Scripture says,

> *"All of Israel from Dan even to Beersheba knew that*
> *Samuel was confirmed as a prophet of the Lord."*

The Lord used His audible voice to help Samuel realize the calling on his life and to establish his spiritual position as prophet over Israel. This story is an example of how God can and will speak with an audible voice at times. It is more common during this dispensation, however, for the Lord to speak with an inner voice. Leanne Payne, author and expert on hearing the voice of God and inner healing, wrote in her book, *Listening Prayer*:

> *"God deeply impresses His inaudible word on our*
> *thoughts through His 'still, small voice.' We know*
> *these are not our thoughts but those from God. This*
> *way of God's speaking can be every whit as powerful*
> *in its effects as the seemingly more dramatic way of*
> *hearing an audible voice, receiving an angelic visitor*
> *or receiving through a phenomenal experience."*

In my experience the "still, small voice" is a frequently used way in which the Lord communicates to those who have the gift of prophecy. In turn, the prophetically gifted often speak forth God's thoughts to others. For example, Lisa—a mother, medical professional and person with the gift of prophecy—recently described how she experiences this "Nabi" flow of communication from the Father:

> *"When the Lord speaks to me or through me, it's like*
> *unction in my spirit and it spouts out of me. I hear the*
> *words within my spirit and mind and then I am*

compelled to speak forth what I hear, walking in faith that what the Lord is telling me is from the well that He has for that person. Often, He will give me insights into that person's life that only He would know—personal hurts or struggles that they have not shared with anyone else. When I speak prophetically, it feels as though the Lord is pouring His words out of me and they spill forth until He has communicated all that He desires to say to that person. When He has communicated all He desires, the words simply stop coming and I know He is done."

The voice of God directs, heals, restores and encourages. It is wonderful to personally hear His voice and know that He cares enough to give voice to His concern for His children.

Dreams

Dreams and visions are documented throughout Scripture; yet within the Body of Christ, they are probably the most disputed type of communication from God. I believe this is due, in part, to the difficulty of accurate interpretations of dreams and visions. I have seen the fruit of God-given dreams and visions in my life and the lives of my students. I believe the Church has entered the season prophesied by the prophet Joel:

And it shall come to pass afterward That I will pour out My Spirit on all flesh; Your sons and your daughters shall prophesy, Your old men shall dream dreams, Your young men shall see visions (Joel 2:28 NKJ). In spite of this passage, many wonder why the Lord would want to speak to believers in dreams and visions, especially dreams that are filled with symbolism and left to our fleshly interpretation. The answer can be found in Job 33:14-17 that says,

"For God may speak in one way, or in another, Yet man does not perceive it. In a dream, in a vision of the night, When deep sleep falls upon men, While slumbering on their beds, Then He opens the ears of men, And seals their instruction in order to turn man from his deed, And conceal pride from man."

A student in the Eagles International Leadership Training School named Nancy recently shared a very vivid dream she had several months ago. She explained she had not had a dream like this before, nor has she had one since. She was walking along a beach with Jesus as He talked about how He wanted to heal her inner hurts. He was also talking about her future ministry. He was teaching her directly from Isaiah 43 and Isaiah 58. About half way through the dream, a dark cloud rushed over the water and she was terrified that it would consume her. Jesus covered her with His robe to protect her until the cloud passed. The Lord's protection on her life was clear.

When Nancy awakened every detail of the dream was crystal clear in her mind. "It was more like I lived the dream than dreamed it," she said. The dream gave her healing, hope and restoration as it fulfilled Numbers 12:6:

"If there is a prophet among you, I, the Lord, will make Myself known to him in a vision; I speak to him in a dream."

Dreams are wonderful avenues through which the Lord can provide warning, hope, healing and restoration. It is important to ask the Lord for His truth and interpretation for each dream He gives, and then walk with intention in the understanding and truth within the interpretation.

Visions

Visions are similar to dreams except they happen when you're awake. Generally there are two types of visions. The first is internal, where you see pictures in your mind, much like a daydream. The second is an open vision, where the picture is played before you almost like a movie. Both types of visions can bring warning, prophetic words, instruction and encouragement.

In her book, *The Voice of God,* internationally known prophet Cindy Jacobs discusses how many people don't realize they're having visions. She says,

> *"The Lord might flash a picture of your child being hurt, which will prompt you to go and find out what the child is doing. Right when you enter the room, you see your five-year-old child standing on the ledge of the window of your two-story house and there is no screen to protect him from falling. You go over and pluck him from danger—just in the nick of time. Some remember the flash picture of the child just before they went to look for him, and others don't realize it was God who gave them the picture of warning."*

Nancie, my friend and armor bearer is a seer. When asked how she uses her gift to minister prophetically, she says,

> *"When I am ministering to someone prophetically, I often get pictures. As my gift has developed and grown, I have become more able to understand what the Lord is saying through the pictures and I work hard to paint a visual for the person I am prophesying over. By painting the picture that I am seeing, they are better able to conceptualize what the Lord is saying to them. It is important for them to understand the broad strokes of what I am seeing as well as the details of the message from the Lord."*

Visions should be heeded and prayed over. Don't credit your imagination for your visions, but take the time to seek the Lord for

His meaning and purpose within the vision. In my experience, visions can be some of the most powerful and life-changing forms of communication from God the Father today.

The Word of Knowledge

Where many prophetic words give vast pictures and often multiple forms of information, a word of knowledge illuminates a specific need or detail. Instead of lengthy words that take many twists and turns, a word of knowledge is often composed of one single word or a short thought. For example, I may hear the word "depression" and know in that moment the Lord wants to heal or minister to someone who is struggling with depression. Often it is someone I do not know, although sometimes it is an individual I know but have been unaware of their struggle

Oftentimes when I hear a word of knowledge I will stop teaching and ask if there is an individual who is struggling with the particular issue that has been brought to mind. I cannot tell you how many times I have done this only to have a person come forward who is truly in need of ministry, healing and the touch of God's love. Once they have been identified, I will pray with them over their needs. I am constantly amazed at how one or two words brought to the mind by the Holy Spirit can bring such healing.

Recently we did an exercise on the word of knowledge while teaching at a school of the prophets in Colorado Springs. I asked the students to share if a specific word had been give to them and how it ministered to their hearts. One student told of the word that had been given about "doubt and fear." *"It confirmed what I had been feeling. It let me know that God is also concerned with my progress enough to assure me that everything will work out in His time,"* she said.

I want to caution you not to limit the power and effectiveness of a word of knowledge because of the brief nature of the Holy Spirit's communication to you. No matter how short, the Lord uses a word of knowledge to touch people in powerful ways and to communicate His Heart, will and direction.

God Speaks Through People

Joni Eareckson Tada is a world renowned author and speaker. Her life was forever changed at age 17 when she broke her neck in a diving accident. In her book, *The God I Love,* she talks about how the Lord used a friend to break through her depression following the accident. She writes,

> *"...then Jacque—my friend, my sharer of milk-shakes, hockey sticks, and boyfriends—climbed into bed next to me. She instinctively knew the only thing that would bring comfort, and in the midst of that dark night, she sang: 'Man of Sorrows!' What a name! For the Son of God who came Ruined sinners to reclaim! Hallelujah, what a savior! That's what Jacque helped me to grasp that night. God didn't give words, he gave the Word - Jesus, the bruised and bloody Man of Sorrows."*

While we cannot fully understand Joni's experience, she eloquently explains how the Lord used her friend Jacque to bring healing and restoration to her weary soul. One of the most magnificent ways in which the Father communicates His abounding love is through people like Jacque who sing loving and caring Holy Spirit led songs!

Regardless of how God speaks, He desires for you to hear Him. Perhaps it's time for you to realize that a lot of your experiences are not happenstance. They are very likely your Father in Heaven talking to you, revealing His truth and bringing His loving direction.

"Father, I thank You for being a God who speaks to Your children in individual and unique ways. I ask You, Father, to reveal to me the ways in which You speak personally to me. Sharpen my ability to hear Your voice and grant me wisdom as I begin to listen for You in new ways. I ask, in the Name of Jesus, as I begin to step out in new ways, that You will grant me Your discernment. Even now I choose to

bind my mind to the mind of Christ so that as I hear You speak, I will clearly recognize and follow Your voice. Thank you, Father. Amen."

Questions
1. List some of the ways God speaks?
2. What ways do you think He may have spoken to you before that you didn't recognize as coming from Him?
3. Will you listen or look for God's voice new ways now that you have read this chapter?
4. Is there a way in which you are sure the Lord has never spoken to you before?
5. What, if any, have been the roadblocks that have prevented you from recognizing the voice of God in the past?

I Think I Heard God Speak–How Do I Really Know It Was Him?

My sheep hear my voice, and I know them, and they
follow me...(John 10:27).

Now that you have a better understanding of how the Lord speaks, it is important to understand that while God would never mislead or deceive you, Satan will *always* try to lead you down a road of lies and deception.

Two modern day examples of people who were used by the enemy to entrap others who sought the voice of God are Jim Jones and David Koresh. Both men claimed to hear the voice of God and multitudes followed them without testing the teaching they were receiving against the Scriptures. Sadly, these people were mislead, manipulated and eventually died as a result of these great deceptions. These tragedies could have been avoided had these people understood that the messages they were hearing did not line up with Scriptures and that they were conforming to the enemy's twisted doctrine.

Man's flesh is fallible and the enemy will use this fallibility to distort, confuse and discourage. Therefore, take note of the warning in I John 4:1:

"Beloved, do not believe every spirit, but test the spirits, whether they are of God; because many false prophets have gone out into the world."

Know the Word

The Bible is the Christian's first line of defense against the enemy's schemes. Any true word from the Lord will *always* align itself with the Scriptures. There is no room to vary on this point. If what you have heard is contrary to the Bible, it must be immediately discarded. It is that simple. Steve Thompson summarizes this in his book, *"You May All Prophesy!"* He states:

"Any prophetic interpretation that contradicts Scripture must be judged as inaccurate. The Bible is our grounding influence and our 'base line' for prophecy. Spoken prophecy should never replace nor supercede our dependence on the written Word for instruction and doctrine."

It is essential for everyone who desires to grow in their personal relationship with God to spend time in the Word. This need will only increase as you begin to grow and develop in the prophetic. Psalms 119:105 says, *"Your word is a lamp to my feet, and a light to my path."* A foundation that is built on the Bible will illuminate your path. Nothing else can illuminate darkness like the Word.

It is important to understand, however, that building a strong foundation takes time and effort. Psalms 119:48 says,

"My hands also I will lift up to Your commandments, Which I love, And I will meditate on Your statutes."

You can only discern God's voice through meditation of His Word and statutes. Bill Hamon describes the process of building a stronger foundation in his book, *Prophets and Personal Prophecy – God's Prophetic Voice Today*. He states:

"To build more, a deeper foundation must be laid for a greater building. And that means we must first tear down the old building, dig up the old, limited foundation, and lay a new one for a ten-story ministry instead of a one-story ministry."

Although Dr. Hamon is referring to building a greater foundation for a growing ministry, you can apply this principle to discerning more clearly and understanding the voice of God. It is only through an ever deepening understanding of God's Word that you can grow in your personal relationship with Him, which includes the ability of hearing Him speak.

Imani, one of the youngest students in my leadership training class, recently talked about building a foundation with the Lord and how in doing so, her ability to hear His voice has grown. She says,

"You need to work earnestly to build a solid foundation on the Word of God. You should ask the Lord to teach you about His heart and His character so that you can enter into the prophetic easier. In my life, the more time I have spent in the Word the better my prophetic gifting has flowed. I'm now better equipped to discern if I am hearing the true voice of God because His Word is imprinted on my heart."

Out of the mouth of a babe comes such wisdom! I cannot implore you enough to begin reading the Bible before you do anything regarding the prophetic. Study it. Pray over it. Work earnestly to build a solid foundation on the Word. Ask the Lord to teach you about His heart and character so that as you enter into the prophetic, you will be able to discern His true voice and heart.

A foundation built on the Word is essential in developing discernment between the Father's voice and that of the enemy. As the Scripture says in I Timothy 4:15:

"Meditate on these things; give yourself entirely to them, that your progress may be evident to all.

Know the Schemes of the Enemy and Counter Them with the Word and the Father's Heart

John Calvin once said, "We must remember that Satan has his miracles, too." This is such a simple, yet profound, statement. Not all prophetic words, miracles, and signs and wonders are from God. The enemy can also conjure up the miraculous. Many believers who have not studied the Scriptures find it hard to believe they can be overcome by Satan's schemes or that he can mimic the Word of God. However, this myth can be easily dispelled by taking a look at the Bible.

The Lord had prepared Moses with several signs and wonders to demonstrate that he was chosen by God *before* he approached Pharaoh. Moses demonstrated many miracles before the king of Egypt, from turning his staff into a snake to changing the water into blood. However, Pharaoh's magicians were also able to duplicate the same miracles through their "secret arts" (Exodus 8:6), which were from the devil. The purpose of these counterfeit wonders were to make God look less powerful in Pharaoh's eyes and gave way for the Lord to harden his heart for His plan and purposes. However, God's power prevailed over the enemy's until the magicians eventually proclaimed:

"This is the finger of God." (Exodus 8:19)

It is important in today's world full New Age teaching, psychics and spiritualism to see the enemy's wonders and teaching for what they are—counterfeits of God's power. Satan has tried hard to look, sound and feel like the voice of God, however, instead of truth, he brings distortion, lies and ultimate destruction. The road of the counterfeit may feel good initially but it is laden with traps and ultimately separation from the living God.

The Apostle Paul foresaw the times we are living in today when he wrote:

"But there were also false prophets among the people, just as there will be false teachers among

*you. They will secretly bring in destructive heresies,
even denying the sovereign Lord who bought them—
bringing swift destruction on themselves. And many
will follow their destructive ways, because of whom
the way of truth to be blasphemed."* (II Peter 2:1-3

Do not be lead astray as you enter into the prophetic and begin
to grow in hearing the voice of God. Allow the Lord to confirm His
truths to you and be diligent to not be as those Paul spoke of in II
Timothy 4:3 when he said, *"For the time will come when they will
not endure sound doctrine, but according to their own desires,
because they have itching ears, they will heap up for themselves
teachers."* Cling to sound doctrine. Be steadfast in testing the spirits
and walk in the freedom you have as you enjoy the blessing of
knowing you are hearing the voice of your heavenly Father!

The Flesh is Weak

Another area believers need to guard is their flesh. The psalmist
David pinpointed this area of weakness when he wrote,
*"My flesh and my heart fail; But God is the strength of my heart
and my portion forever"* (Psalms 73:26 NKJV). There is no doubt
that you can fall into temptation because of your sinful nature and
fleshly desires. Therefore, it is important to diligently examine all
that you hear to ensure it is not your flesh that is leading you astray.
In his book *How to Listen to God,* Charles Stanley writes:

> *"If what we hear urges us to gratify the flesh, to
> forget what anyone else says, just do as we please,
> then we should know that it isn't of God. He doesn't
> speak in those terms. God always speaks in such a
> way that the results please the Spirit of God within
> us, not the flesh."*

An example of how the flesh can distort God's truth can be
found in the book, *"Five Steps to Financial Freedom* by James

Wise, a Christian financial planner:

> *"I remember a counseling situation many years ago in which a friend was seeking God's leading in how to reduce debt and begin to save regularly. These goals were very consistent with biblical principles. While pursuing these specific goals, however, a severe lack of contentment quickly set in. The next time I saw my friend he was driving a new car. Not only was the new loan amount considerably larger than the old loan, the loss on the old car—which had been running just fine, by the way—had been rolled into the new loan. The result of this transaction: Total debt had increased and cash flow worsened. Sometimes we start out by seeking God's leading, but then we get tired of waiting and take matters into our own hands. It is always easy for us to say, 'God led me to do this,' but God doesn't provide direction that violates His own principles. In the case I just described, the goal to buy a new car could not possibly have come from the Lord."*

It would be easy to say, "I heard the voice of God say do this or that," when in reality it was your flesh. I have seen both prophetically experienced Christians and those who are new to the prophetic give into these fleshly desires, but it is important for you to walk as the Apostle Paul explained in Romans 8:5:

> *"For those who live according to the flesh, set their minds on the things of the flesh, but those who live according to the Spirit, the things of the Spirit"*

When your mind, thoughts, hopes and desires are rooted in the foundation of the Word, then you will be able to discern what is truly from God and what is not.

When you ask God for bread, He will not give you a stone (Luke 11:11). Therefore, you can rest knowing that while there are pitfalls of the enemy and your flesh, the Lord will equip and guide you all as you seek His voice and direction. Quin Sherrer, an author, teacher and friend, addresses this issue in her book *"Listen God is Speaking to You."* She records a prayer that can help you in the area of your flesh:

> *"If you have difficulty discerning which voice it might be, you may want to say a prayer like this: "Lord, I desire to hear Your voice and be led by You. If this is Your Holy Spirit speaking, please cause this impression I have to become more clear and urgent. If this impression is not of You, please cause it to fade. By the authority of the blood of Jesus that covers me, I address any evil spirits present and command them to be silent in Jesus' name. I will listen only to the voice of my Shepherd. Thank You Father, for speaking to me by whatever means You choose as I wait upon You."*

I want to encourage all who want to hear God's voice to take a moment and pray this prayer. Then take a moment to listen for His voice. Compare the word that you hear from the Lord against the character of God that is described in the Bible:

> *"For I know the thoughts that I think toward you, says the LORD, thoughts of peace and not of evil, to give you a future and a hope"* (Jeremiah 29:11).

Remember, God will *never* lead you down a path that is contrary to His sanctification process. His Words will *always be life giving* and will work for your good. If the word you've received does these two things, then pray over it and ask the Lord for revelation. Next, take the necessary steps to fulfill the word and then *rest,* knowing that God loves you enough to communicate His plans for your life.

"Dear Lord, I thank You that You are all powerful, all knowing, and everywhere. I praise You that You desire to speak to me and although

my flesh is weak and the enemy schemes against me, You are stronger and able to help me overcome. Please direct my steps and grant me discernment to know when You are speaking. Also Father, fill me with your boldness so that when You speak and direct I will go forth and obey. Thank You Father, for all You are doing. I praise You that You love me enough to speak personally to me! Amen."

Questions:
1. What are some schemes that Satan uses to mimic God's voice?
2. What is a biblical example of a counterfeit wonder?
3. Have you ever thought you heard the voice of God but realized it was not His voice? Did you test the spirits at the time?
4. What will you do differently now when you hear the voice of God?

The Holy Spirit is Our Helper

"These things I have spoken to you while being present with you. But the Helper, the Holy Spirit, whom the Father will send in My name, He will teach you all things, and bring to your remembrance all things that I said to you". John 14:26

Think of a time you were involved in making a decision that would affect your family. Perhaps it was a critical decision regarding medical treatment for a loved one, or maybe you had considered a career change that would have caused you to move across the country. Big decisions can be grueling, especially when the well being of your loved ones is at stake.

My family has faced many difficult situations, and we've found each decision we've had to make as challenging as the one before. Yet, knowing the Holy Spirit was there to guide us gave us the freedom to walk boldly through the decision-making process as we walked down those difficult roads. I'm sure you have also experienced the Holy Spirit's touch throughout your journey with the Lord, although you may not have recognized His presence.

The Holy Spirit—the Lesser?

Perhaps you've had thoughts that you perceived as your own when in reality they were placed in your heart and mind by the Holy Spirit. I challenge you to think of those "intuitions" or "gut feelings" you've experienced in the past as coming from the Holy Spirit. He has provided important insight that moved you beyond your personal discernment or common sense.

One reason I believe so many believers miss the voice of the Holy Spirit is because they do not understand Who He is. They have relegated the Him to a position of the lesser member of the Trinity. The Holy Spirit is seen as little more than an impersonal, influential force that lacks the attributes manifested by the other two members of the Trinity—God the Father and God the Son. This is not true of course. The Holy Spirit is an equal part of the Triune God. He has feelings and personality traits, such as a mind, will and emotions. He is referred to in Scriptures as a Counselor, Helper, Intercessor, Advocate, Strengthener and Standby. He is all-powerful, all knowing, ever present and eternal. He is moral, often called the Spirit of holiness, the Spirit of Truth and the Spirit of love. The Holy Spirit is God and God is abounding, endless. He is the very essence of true love.

In his book *"Spurgeon on the Holy Spirit,"* Charles Spurgeon writes:

> *"Let me tell you of the love of the Spirit for you and me. Oh, how early was that love that He manifested toward us, even in our childhood! My friends, we can well remember how the Spirit was inclined to reach us. We went astray from the womb, speaking lies, but how early did the Spirit of God stir up our consciences and solemnly correct us because of our youthful sins! How frequently since then has the Spirit wooed us! How often under the ministry has He compelled our hearts to melt and tears to run down our cheeks! He has sweetly whispered in our ears, 'My child, give Me your heart. Go to your*

room, shut the door behind you, confess your sins, and seek the Savior's love and blood.'"

Just as God the Father and God the Son are intimately involved in every believer's life, God the Holy Spirit is too. And just as God the Father and His Son Jesus Christ desire a relationship with all believers, the Holy Spirit desires to know, love, speak to and direct every believer. Benny Hinn describes the Holy Spirit in his book *"Good Morning, Holy Spirit,"* as

"The most beautiful, most precious, loveliest person on the earth." I cannot help but agree. The Holy Spirit is my Friend, love, hope, helper and guide. You should keep in mind, however, that while the Holy Spirit is a Person, He is not a man. He always has been and always will be God. He is perfect and holy in every way. You should to approach Him with reverence and in the fear of God."

King David displayed reverence and fear of the godhead. He is referred to in Scriptures as a man "after God's own heart" because he sought a relationship not only with God the Father, but also with the Holy Spirit. When sin separated David from the presence of the Holy Spirit, he pleaded with the Father to

"Cast me not away from thy presence; and take not thy Holy Spirit from me."

King David was desperate for the Holy Spirit. It is my prayer that all believers might learn from the king's passion for the Lord and to desire the Holy Spirit as he did.

What is the state of your relationship with the Holy Spirit? Are you passionate about a relationship with Him or have you relegated Him to being the lesser of the triune God? Isn't it time to open your heart to the Third and equally important Member of the Trinity? Why don't you pause and pray this prayer:

"God the Holy Spirit, I am coming to You today to ask for Your forgiveness. I didn't know that You desire a relationship with me. That it was Your heart's desire to commune with me, know me, love me and guide me. I am sorry that I have pushed You into a mold where You should have never been. Please forgive me and reveal Yourself to me. Open my eyes to the truth of Who You are and develop deep within me a godly passion to know and serve You. I ask You to fill me, teach me, comfort me, guide me, convict me and sanctify me. Holy Spirit, teach me to hear Your voice and help me to know You better. I desire to worship You and praise You in every way. Fill me anew, Holy Spirit, and return to me the joy of my salvation. I want to love You and know You more and more each day. Amen."

How the Holy Spirit Helps

We see examples throughout the Bible of how the Holy Spirit is an active, vital participant in the lives of God's children. Let's take a few moments to look at a few specific examples.

Giving Wisdom and Granting Favor

Daniel is one of our greatest biblical figures. He was taken captive at an early age and taken to a foreign land where he was held as a prisoner of war, separated from his family and the traditions of his people. In spite of his captivity, however, Daniel sought the Lord and stayed committed to His commands.

The Lord blessed Daniel's steadfastness and the Holy Spirit poured Himself upon him. His presence was so strong in Daniel's life that he was able to interpret dreams that no one else in the kingdom could explain. The divine wisdom and knowledge the Holy Spirit revealed to Daniel caused King Belshazzar to declare:

"The Spirit of God is in you, and that light and understanding and excellent wisdom are found in you" (Daniel 5:14). Daniel was promoted to positions of honor in the land of his captivity because *"...an excellent spirit was in him."*

Isn't it amazing and encouraging that the same Holy Spirit is working within you?

The Holy Spirit Gives Boldness and Provides the Words

The transforming power of the Holy Sprit comes into full manifestation in the New Testament, as is evidenced when He brought astounding boldness to Peter when he spoke before the Sanhedrin Council:

"Then *Peter, filled with the Holy Spirit, said to them, 'Rulers of the people and elders of Israel: If we this day are judged for a good deed done to a helpless man, by what means he has been made well, let it be known to you all, and to all the people of Israel, that by the name of Jesus Christ of Nazareth, whom you crucified, whom God raised from the dead, by Him this man stands here before you whole. This is the 'stone which was rejected by you builders, which has become the chief cornerstone.' Nor is there salvation in any other, for there is no other name under heaven given among men by which we must be saved"* (Acts 4:8-12).

Members of the Sanhedrin knew Peter and John were uneducated men, yet they could not help but "marvel" at Peter's words. After talking amongst themselves, they decided to release Peter and John on the condition that they not speak or teach in the name of Jesus anymore. However, the Holy Spirit moved upon them again as they responded in unison:

*"Whether it is right in the sight of God to give heed
to you rather than to God, you be the judge; for we
cannot stop speaking what we have seen and heard."*

Likewise, the Holy Spirit can fill you with boldness to speak
when you are accused.

The Holy Spirit Can Fill You with Mercy and Forgiveness in Inexplicable Ways

Another example of the power of the Holy Spirit in a believer's
life is found in Acts 6. Stephen, who is described as a disciple
"filled with faith and the Holy Spirit" (Acts 6:8), was falsely
accused of blasphemy in an attempt to destroy the work he was
doing through the power of the Holy Spirit. Instead of becoming
fearful or angry, the Holy Spirit rested upon him and he, like Peter
and John, spoke with great boldness as he said:

*"You stiff necked and uncircumcised in heart and
ear! You always resist the Holy Spirit; as your
fathers did, so do you."* Enraged, the crowd began to
stone him. Remarkably, even as he was being
stoned, Stephen cried out with a loud voice, *"Lord
do not charge them with this sin."* And then he died.

No one without the power of the Holy Spirit could demonstrate
such forgiveness and compassion. It was the power of the Holy
Spirit that enabled Stephen to love his murderers. The touch of the
Holy Spirit is amazing. Whether He is granting great wisdom, boldness or mercy; the power and influence of the Holy Spirit is something I desire to always be present in my life.

D. L. Moody once said, "God commands us to be filled with the
Spirit; and if we aren't filled, it's because we're living beneath our
privileges." Do you desire to be filled with the Holy Spirit? It
doesn't matter whether you're Evangelical or Charismatic, take a
moment and ask the Lord to reveal Himself to you in a new way.

Ask the Holy Spirit to fill you anew so that He can lead, guide and help you with all that you need to do.

It is important to understand that the Holy Spirit manifests Himself in different ways. Sometimes He moves softly and tenderly. In her book, *"Experiencing God in Prayer,"* Madame Jeanne Guyon, a woman held in high esteem by 18th century Christian leaders, said *"Don't hurry into other forms of prayer when you are quiet before God. Simply allow yourself time to enjoy His presence and be filled full in your spirit."* The most intimate moments I've experienced with the Holy Spirit have occurred as I've waited quietly before Him and allowed Him to minister to me. I know many others who experience Him the same way.

Jean, a strong, intercessor who has served the Lord as a missionary for almost 40 years, spends a great deal of time listening for the Lord. She explains,

> *"I find waiting on God in silence often draws me near to God in intangible ways. He ministers His presence to me. I may experience an overwhelming sense of His presence, which softens my heart and draws me to Him in love. Or I may experience awe, which causes me to lie prostrate on the floor just worshiping Him. His Presence may draw me to rest in silence like a weaned child on his mother's breast, enjoying nurture and love. To wait on God in silence is to be in a 'receiving mode'...receiving His love, acceptance, delight in me, His holiness, adequacy or sufficiency. It is a time to commune with Him in love, not with activity, but awareness of Him alone. Tears may result out of an overflow of gratefulness for such overwhelming grace and kindness experienced in His presence. Therefore, silence is not 'deadness.' It is full of activity, but the activity of the Lord's choosing."*

At times the Holy Spirit moves quietly and tenderly. You will experience your most intimate times of fellowship when you take time to wait silently before Him. The Holy Spirit will connect your heart to God's and help you hear His voice. Zephaniah 3:17 says:

> *"The LORD your God is in your midst, The Mighty*
> *One, will save; He will rejoice over you with glad-*
> *ness, He will quiet you with His love, He will rejoice*
> *over you with singing."*

The Holy Spirit desires to be as active and present in your life today as He was 2000 years ago. Just as the apostles listened for and responded to His guidance, you should be doing the same.

You will need the Holy Spirit in every circumstance of your life. He is a precious gift from God. Allow Him to help you. Listen for His voice and guidance. Ask Him to fill and teach you in every way and never forget to say, *"Thanks be to God for His indescribable gift"* (II Corinthians 9:15).

> *God the Holy Spirit, thank You for loving me and*
> *being involved in every aspect of my life. Teach me,*
> *develop me and fill me. Help me to hear Your voice*
> *and direct all the days of my life. Amen*

Questions
1. How does the Holy Spirit help you?
2. Have you relegated the Holy Spirit the position of the lesser of the triune God? Has your opinion changed after reading this chapter?
3. Have you only expected the Holy Spirit to move powerfully in your life? Can you now see other ways in which He moves?
4. What is your favorite biblical example of the Holy Spirit as the believer's helper?

How Can I Learn to Prophesy?

Or if he asks for an egg, will he offer him a
scorpion?" (Luke 11:12).

I would encourage anyone who is interested in developing in prophecy to look for classes where they can grow in a biblically based and safe environment. In my opinion, any prophetic class must be taught with the spirit of I Corinthians 14:1-3, where the love of the Father is paramount and all prophecy given is for the edification, exhortation and comfort the hearers.

That being said, many have asked me how they can learn to hear the voice of God and prophesy if there aren't classes in their community or smalls groups in their church. Take heart! According to I John 2:27, if Jesus Christ is your Savior then the anointing of the Holy Spirit *will teach you*. In fact, this is what happened in my life.

My prophetic gift began to grow and develop years ago when I was involved in several home Bible study groups. As I grew in Christ and began to hear clearly His voice, I realized I was hearing the Father's voice for those I was studying with. Although initially it was scary to step out, I began to share with my friends what I was hearing.

As time passed I saw the fruit of the prophetic words I was sharing with individuals and began to share more freely. To my excitement, each time I gave a word, the Holy Spirit taught me something new. Before I knew it, my ability to hear and discern the voice of the Lord had increased significantly and the words I gave were even more accurate than before. Why? Because the Holy Spirit—my Teacher—was helping me grow and develop in greater discernment and understanding. Without a doubt, the principle of the parable of the talents was being lived out in my life. Each time I used the talents the Lord had given, He freely gave more. I am excited to say, the same can be true for you.

Before I go any further, let me say that you should not abuse the spiritual gifts. While I am very supportive of Christians ministering prophetically, I *do not* believe they should have prophecy parties where the gifts become a reason to socialize. You should receive the gift of prophecy wholeheartedly and merrily. At the same time, however, you must govern it...*take care of it*...and not abuse this precious and intimate form of communication from our Father in Heaven..

Understanding the depth of reverence that must be given to this spiritual gift, we can now discuss how you can learn to prophesy. As I have said before, it is essential to first root yourself in the Word of God before you move into the prophetic. Without a growing understanding of the Scriptures it will be easy to be deceived by the enemy. I feel it is necessary to reiterate that before you move any further into the prophetic you must first establish yourself in the Word and daily seek a relationship with God.

It is also important to be of a pure heart and mind. Just as you approach communion with reverence, you should approach listening for the voice of the Father with a humble and contrite heart. It is only through His mercy and love that you will be able to commune with Him. For this reason, allow the Lord to search your heart and reveal any areas that need repentance and restoration. The Lord speaks of this in Isaiah 66:2:

> *"This is the one I esteem: he who is humble and contrite in spirit, and trembles at my word.*

Your deepest desire should be to be right before the Lord. He will speak to you without boundaries and barriers when you approach Him with a pure heart. It is only then that the enemy is weakened and you are better able to hear His voice.

Take a moment now and ask God to show you any areas that He wants you to surrender to Him. Confess the sins that He brings to your mind, remembering I John 1:9, which says,

> *"If we confess our sins, he is faithful and just and will forgive us our sins and purify us from all unrighteousness."*

After time in the Word, confession and restoration with the Lord, I would encourage you to "stir up the gifts" by praying in the Holy Spirit. If you do not have the gift of tongues, I suggest that you *"Enter his gates with thanksgiving and his courts with praise; give thanks to him and praise his name"* (Psalms 100:4). And finally, come before the Lord *believing* that you can hear His voice and wait on Him to speak.

Prophetic Activation Exercises

I have mentioned the prophetic classes I teach. I would like to take a moment now to explain several prophetic activation exercises that I administer during these classes. These exercises are designed to build up the participant's faith and to demonstrate that they are equipped and able to hear and speak forth the voice of God.

Since these exercises are done through the prophetic anointing brought by the Holy Spirit, each Word given must be given according to Paul's council in I Corinthians 14:3:

> *"But he who prophesies speaks edification and exhortation and comfort to men."*

At no time should anyone who is participating in these activations give a word of doom and gloom, direction, correction or discipline. Doing so would be out of the boundaries given in this Scripture.

As we enter into this portion of teaching it is my prayer that your spiritual ears will open in the Name of Jesus, your mind will be bound to the mind of Christ, and that the Holy Spirit will come with His prophetic anointing to touch and teach you.

You will need at least one partner for these prophetic activations. I often encourage people who are not well acquainted to partner up so there is no confusion that the words they are getting are from the Holy Spirit and not their friends. If however, your partner is someone you know intimately, ask the Lord to bring forth a word that is unique and outside of the realm that you know about.

Blessing Prayer

The first activation that I teach is a prayer of blessing. In these prayers, no terminology such as "Thus says the Lord" or "I hear the voice of the Lord saying" should be used. It is a prayer where you allow the Holy Spirit to lead you to bless and touch the very heart of the person you are praying over. Below is an example of a prayer of blessing. This is just an *example* and you should allow the Holy Spirit to lead you as you pray for your partner.

> *"Lord, I thank you for Sarah. I bless her with Your strength, love and tenderness. I thank You, Father, that You have her hidden and protected in Your quiver against the plans and schemes of the enemy. I thank You Father that You are bringing her into a new season—and though the season is filled with change and sometimes pain—that You are in the midst of that pain holding her, loving her and protecting her. I thank You Father that she is precious and beloved in Your sight. I praise You that You have never left her or forsaken her. I pray that the truth of Your love and mercy toward her would be evident and clear at the depths of her heart even today. I pray all of this in the Name of Jesus. Amen.*

This is a simple prayer, but one I believe will edify and comfort the receiver, especially since it comes from the heart of the Father. Take a moment before moving on to pray a blessing over your partner. After you have prayed over them, allow them to take a moment to pray over you.

Facing the Wall

This activation is typically done with a large group of people. It will not work in a group of only two, although it is possible to do in a group of four. Begin by having the people number off "one, two, one, two" until everyone in the group has a number. Then ask all of the number "ones" to stand with their faces toward the wall, and the number "twos" to stand behind someone in the "ones" group *without saying a word*. The person who is facing the wall should have no knowledge of who is behind them. (I encourage those facing the wall to pray in tongues, but the person who is standing behind them must be silent.)

After a moment the person who is standing behind the other participant is instructed to touch the person facing the wall on the shoulder. The touch is brief and only to indicate to the person who is facing the wall that they are in position and ready for the prophecy. After another moment of silence with the Lord, I instruct the person facing the wall to begin to speak what they believe they are hearing from the Father. Frequently students have walked into this activation with great trepidation and doubt. I have heard some say, "This is impossible." And my response is always the same: "Nothing is impossible for our God."

As the activation takes place I am always delighted to see my students stepping out in faith. Though they don't know whom they are giving a prophetic word to and may be fearful of saying something wrong, I can't think of one time where the anointing of the Holy Spirit has not come and blessed them.

After a few moments, I have those who just given a prophetic word turn around to see who they prophesied to. More often than not, they are surprised to discover that the person who stood behind has just been touched by the Lord in a mighty way through them. In one memorable class, a student whom I will call Danielle was very skeptical about the prophecy she was about to deliver. As she faced the wall she believed without a shadow of a doubt that the person behind her was a woman, yet the words she heard in her spirit applied to a man. As she gave the prophetic word she imagined how offended the "woman" behind her must be, yet to her surprise when she turned around a man was standing behind her crying, saying, "One-hundred percent! One-hundred percent of everything I have been asking the Lord to confirm to me!"

Danielle's skepticism was forever removed. She now believes she can hear the voice of God and regularly engages in speaking forth words of exhortation, comfort and edification as the Spirit leads.

Circle in a Circle

The final activation should be used in a large group setting. Once again, I have the class number off, "one, two, one, two" until everyone in the class has a number. Then, I have each group form a circle—one, circle within the other—the inner circle facing out and the outer circle facing in so each person is paired and looking at someone from the opposite circle.

Before the activation begins one of the circles is delegated as the "giving" circle and the other is the "receiving" circle. (For the purposes of this explanation, the outside circle will be the "giving" and the inside will be the "receiving".) When the exercise begins, the person on the outside will begin to speak forth whatever the Holy Spirit brings to mind. This exercise is quick moving and there is not a great deal of time to think about what is going to be said. This is important because so often we rely on our physical senses when we speak prophetically instead of relying on the Holy Spirit.

After about 20 seconds, I call out "change" and both circles shift the opposite direction, which pairs up new partnerships. Again, the person on the outside must speak forth what they are hearing the Holy Spirit say *very quickly* because there is only a short time before I call out "change" again.

Once the circle has rotated through and everyone in the inner circle has received a short prophetic word from everyone on the outside, we then switch so that those on the outside now are the "receivers" while those on the inside are the "givers." As amazing as it sounds, most people who participate in the "circle in a circle" activation come out of it saying that they heard consistent prophetic words from the Lord from most of the participants, which is proof positive that the Holy Spirit is running the exercise and not me.

I encourage you to practice and use these activations in your Bible studies or church groups to grow your faith in your ability to hear the voice of the Father and in your ability to speak clearly what you are hearing

Taking Action

Once you have heard a prophetic word it is important to understand that there may be some final steps you must take to bring what has been prophesied to completion. First, it is always important to pray over the word that has been given. At my school, prophecies are always tape-recorded. We ask that anyone who receives a prophetic word take the tape home, listen to it, pray over it, write it out seeking the Lord's interpretation and continued revelation about what He said.

It is also important to seek the Lord regarding any action He requires of you to facilitate the fulfillment of the prophecy. As I have mentioned previously, many prophecies that people believe were false were actually true but the recipients never acted with intent regarding them, and therefore, the prophecies did not come to pass. Christine is an example of someone who heard the voice of the Father but needed to take action and obey. Christine had worked in a stressful and demanding position for six years. The load at times was more than any one person could handle and she wanted to leave her job, yet she knew the Lord had brought given her that position and she needed clear direction from the Him before she could leave. During one of my prophetic classes, an individual Christine did not know spoke a prophetic word to her during a class exercise. He said, "Christine, God says, that He would like you to stay in your current job position and if you do, He will bring increase." This word was an answer to Christine's pleas for clear direction.

Christine had to make a decision. She could obey God and remain on her job, or she could leave. Fortunately, she obeyed God and was blessed by the Lord. Within days of the prophetic word, she was given a significant raise and over the last year has been blessed with several bonuses, another raise and great favor. It took action on Christine's part—she had to obey God, but look at the wonderful blessings that followed her.

It is important for anyone who receives a prophecy to understand that according to I Corinthians 13:9

"We know in part and we prophesy in part"

This means that no single prophecy can be viewed as a complete picture or the total answer. Instead, each prophecy must be seen as part of the picture that the Lord is painting to bring completeness, direction and fulfillment into the individual's life.

When you learn how to listen for God's voice, and understand the basic parameters for prophecy and the fact that prophecy is only part of the whole, you will be better able to function under and through this anointing. Praise the Lord that we can all hear His voice and learn how to prophesy. Through reading of the Word, the anointing of the Holy Spirit and a willingness to try, each of us can grow and develop in this area.

"Father, in the Name of Jesus I ask that You would teach this reader how to hear Your voice and prophesy! I ask Holy Spirit that You would bring Your prophetic anointing and give them the grace and ability to speak forth Your very heart for others. I bind the enemy away from this person in the Name of Jesus and proclaim that just as Paul desired that all would prophesy—this person would walk in faith and speak boldly for You! In the Name of Jesus. Amen."

Questions
1. Do you have to attend special classes to learn to prophesy?
2. How does the Apostle Paul instruct all to speak prophetically?
3. Did you try any of the activations? If so, what were the results?
4. How should people respond to individual prophecies?
5. Is action required to fulfill a Word from the Lord?

What If I Make A Mistake When I Prophesy?

"Judge not, and you shall not be judged. Condemn not, and you shall not be condemned. Forgive, and you will be forgiven" (Luke 6:37).

Imagine two parents who are encouraging their toddler to walk. They are clapping and cheering with broad smiles across their faces. As a result of their prompting, their little one gathers up enough courage to stand to his or her feet. Then, with a burst of energy begins to walk toward his or her parents—smiling, giggling, and proud of each step. Then, as suddenly as the walking began, the toddler falls down and begins to cry.

How do you think the parents will react? Will they say, "You're stupid. Can't you walk yet? Get up off that floor right now. You made a big mistake by falling and you're going to pay for it now." *Surely not.* The parents would lovingly pick up their little one, kiss any sore spots and then, encourage him or her to try again with the hope that he or she would go a little bit farther the next time and would soon be able to walk. It is the same in our walk with the Lord. Only God is infallible. Every person who has ever walked the earth is fallible. Why? Because God created you this way. He understands that you may stumble and fall as you press toward the high mark of Christ Jesus. Thankfully, God is always there, waiting to pick you up, kiss the sore spots and encourage you to try again.

If God can show you grace when you make mistakes, surely as brothers and sisters in Christ you can do the same. Unfortunately, when it comes to prophecy—interpreting the mind and will of God—people expect perfection and are quick to find fault. Instead of judging the prophetic word, they judge the prophet. Brothers and sisters, this is not scriptural.

We know from previously examining Isaiah 66:2, that the condition for God's esteem is not perfection, rather the Lord esteems those who have humble and contrite hearts. Therefore, if a prophecy is given with the heart that God desires, yet an error is made, you need to approach the situation according to I Peter 5:6 which says,

> *"Therefore humble yourselves under the mighty hand of God, that He may exalt you in due time,* (NKJV). As you humble yourself, it is important to follow the guidance found in James 5:16:

> *"Confess your trespasses to one another, and pray for one another, that you may be healed. The effective, fervent prayer of a righteous man avails much"*

By admitting your inaccuracy, seeking forgiveness and praying for healing, you will not only preserve your esteem in the eyes of the Father, but you will also bring healing to the person to whom the error was made. For example, a lady came to me several years ago who wanted a touch from God. She had not yet learned that she could hear His voice and deeply desired to hear a word of encouragement. I had been ministering for several days with very few breaks or times of refreshing. Although I was weary, I could see that she needed encouragement, so I prophesied over her.

She contacted me a few days later and said she felt I had not given her an accurate word. I asked her to allow me to hear the tape recording of the prophecy so we could go over it together. Unfortunately she had thrown away the tape so we were unable to examine the issue any further. I was unable to remember the specifics of the word, which hindered me from addressing the specifics of the situation. I needed to reach out to her humbly and apologize for what she perceived as a word of error. When I asked for her forgiveness, she graciously accepted and our dialogue opened the door for me to minister to her many more times since this incident. Each time, the Lord has received all the glory for the wonderful things He has used me to speak into her life.

The key to responding to such a situation is love. In fact, the call to walk in and respond with the love of Christ is supreme in any situation regarding any gifts, any ministries and any facet of your life. When you do this, you accomplish Jesus' commandment found in John 13:34-35 which says,

> *"A new commandment I give to you, that you love one another; as I have loved you, that you also love one another. By this all will know that you are My disciples, if you have love for one another."*

By walking in love, you place yourself in the position of being equipped by the Lord. He will never be able to equip you if you are afraid of being wrong. All the Lord is asking for is your willingness to speak when called and for a heart that is willing to learn from mistakes. When you are willing to be God's mouthpiece and to put the fear of failure aside, you become just like the toddler who is learning to walk.

Prophetic Protocol

Knowing that God is encouraging you every step of the way is such a comfort. Yet, since you are fallible and can make mistakes, it is important to establish strong protocols from which to operate and submit. As I have stressed many times, the first consideration for any area in the prophetic is the Scriptures. It is your foundation and reference point. We have established several protocols in my ministry that I believe are scriptural and compassionate.

Protocol No. 1: Care and Wisdom Must Be Exercised at all Times

Imagine for a moment a situation where a prophet is given revelation regarding the status of a person's finance. There is an issue of sin in this individual's life, and because of their gifting this sin has been revealed to the spirit of the prophet. Instead of using care and wisdom, the prophet steps forward and calls the individual forward proclaiming, "The Lord your God has revealed you are in sin. Your finances are in a shambles and you are not being a good steward of your money." The person receiving the word is rendered to tears and brought to great shame through the prophet's actions. However, the prophet believes he is carrying out the work of the Lord and continues on with his ministry without thinking about the devastation he has left behind.

Unfortunately scenarios just like this one have taken place all over the world. Surely you can see that bringing devastation to the lives of God's children is not His will. In fact, such behavior is contrary to Jesus' command in John 15:12: *"This is My commandment, that you love one another as I have loved you."* For this reason, even if the Holy Spirit does reveal sin in a person's life, they should never be called out and embarrassed. Prophetic ministers should never humiliate or shame people. Rather, care should be taken to use terms that are life giving, non critical or exposing. For example, had the prophet called the person forward and instead of tearing them down said something like,

> *"The Lord is calling you to even greater levels of good stewardship. The Holy Spirit desires for all of His children to obey and he is saying that He will equip you, teach you and guide you through the maze of finances you are in. He loves you and will help you—He wants you to submit. In the Scriptures the Lord says, Cast all your cares on him—and He is calling you to do this. So in the Name of Jesus, I call forth the blessing of good stewardship and freedom in this area for this beloved child of God."*

The word of the Lord is still given, however, the conviction of the spirit is left up to the Holy Spirit. The person who has received the word has been built up and encouraged, the word was life-giving and the love of the Father has shone through.

Protocol No. 2: No Parking Lot Prophecies Please

I often hear of individuals who frequently give prophetic words in parking lots or in the back of the church. Frequently those who attend the church have a high level of respect for the person's ability to prophesy; yet become fearful when they see this person headed their way because sometimes their words are discouraging. This type of scenario has developed because many churches have rejected the prophetic and relegated many who are prophetically gifted to a life of operating in secret. As a result, these people have fallen into doom and gloom and speak dark cloud prophecies that are not in alignment with I Corinthians 14:3.

We do not allow people to give prophetic words without training, equipping and a firm understanding of the structure of prophecies, which is for edification, exhortation and comfort. All prophetic words should be tape recorded, not only for the benefit of the receiver, but also for the protection of the one who is giving the word. Then if an error has been made, it can be address and restoration can be made. Without such a back up, accusations and misunderstanding occur and the enemy can cause division and hard feelings. Prophecy, while often private, should never be hidden or without accountability.

Protocol No. 3: Ask First

In a world where people have been hurt and abused, touching and intimate conversations can be perceived as frightening and invasive. Many who operate in the prophetic realm, however, tend to be touchy/feely. The person giving the prophecy must be sensitive to the receiver, who may not want to be touched. Sadly, many offenses have occurred because a prophetic minister has reached out in compassion and touched someone who is wounded and ended up causing more wounding without realizing it. I cannot encourage you enough to not touch people unless you have asked first. If they say it's OK to touch them, to hold their hand or put your hand on their shoulder, by all means do so. However, if they seem uncomfortable or indicate they would prefer not to be touched, do not take offense but rather love them through your words and gestures.

God created touch for the believer's personal enjoyment, but the enemy has defiled it, turning this gesture into something perceived as wounding and wrought with pain. It is imperative for all who minister to be sensitive and aware that although touching can be a wonderful gift, not everyone views it as such.

Will God Manifest Himself and Bring Fresh Revelation for my Life?

" He who has My commandments and keeps them, it is he who loves Me. And he who loves Me will be loved by My Father, and I will love him and manifest Myself to him" (John 14:21)

M any believe prophecy is limited to confirming what God has already spoken to them. They say, "If God wants me to know something, He will tell me Himself and use you to confirm what he is saying." This is a fallacy in the Body of Christ.

God often speaks His purpose, plan and direction through prophetic words because He knows that His children don't often recognize the potential He has placed in them. Through the spirit of prophecy, He can birth and create understanding and direction that will lead you to what He has created and destined you to do. For instance, the first prophecy I ever received was about many of the things that I am doing today. At the time, however, I was a stay-at-home mom with four small children. I was doing well just getting them to school during the week and to church on Sundays and Wednesdays. Thoughts of ministering, teaching the Word and speaking prophetically had never crossed my mind. In fact, at the time the prophecy was given it didn't sound like anything God had ever spoken to me. If anything, it looked off base and I wondered how it could be true. However, I look back on that prophecy today and see that I have now fulfilled the word given and am experiencing it in even greater levels.

The Lord knew I needed direction—direction that would enable me to pursue, grow and develop in my calling—many years ago. God used a prophetic word that brought new revelation and set my feet solidly on the pathway He desired for me. In doing so, Psalms 138:8 was fulfilled in my life:

> *"The Lord will perfect that which concerns me; Your mercy, O Lord, endures forever."*

God manifesting Himself and bringing fresh revelation is not unique to my life. It can be seen in Scripture. For example, there is no record that God had spoken to David about him becoming king over Israel until Samuel prophesied it to him. In fact, David was content tending to his father's sheep until Samuel prophesied God's will and destiny for him. The prophecy was fresh and life changing. First Samuel 16:13 says that after he was anointed by Samuel,

> *"The Spirit of the Lord came upon David from that day forward"*

Despite the tremendous call and anointing upon his life, David responded with humility and a servant's heart when he was called to minister with his harp and lyre before King Saul, the very person he knew he had been anointed to replace.

David's reaction should be an example to all of us. When a prophetic word is given and is in line with the Scriptures, you should believe it, pray over it and move toward it as the Lord leads. You should also remember God's call for you to love and serve others. Whether it takes three days, three weeks, three months or three years for the prophecy to come to pass, you need to remember that God's Word is true and His commands are sure. This means, as you wait on the Lord's timing, you must take the posture that David did and serve wherever the Lord calls.

Isn't it exciting to understand that God speaks to His children and brings new guidance and hope through prophetic words? He is the only One Who knows the plans He has for you. He is your Creator and knows the very purpose for which you were born. Rejoice now. Be glad. Your heavenly Father loves you so much that He wants to speak with you and *with confidence* have you hear His loving voice. Whether you're a child who has lost his way, or a child who has never left His side, the King of Kings and Lord of Lords loves you, knows you, and thinks of you always!

Rest in Him. Seek Him. Draw close to Him. Listen for His voice. He is there and He will never fail to speak to you, lead you and draw you close to Him.

Bibliography

Walter A Elwell, Phd, Philip W. Comfort, Phd. Tyndale Bible Dictionary. Wheaton Illinois: Tyndale 2001

James Stong LL.D., S.T.D, John R. Kohlenberger III, James A. Swanson. The Strongest Strong's Exhaustive Concordance of the Bible. Grand Rapids, Michigan: Zondervan 2001

Grahame Cooke. Developing Your Prophetic Gifting. Grand Rapids, Michigan: Chosen Books 1994 and 2003

Dr. Bill Hamon. Prophets and Personal Prophecy, God's Prophetic Voice Today. Shippensburg, PA: Destiny Image Publishers, Inc 1987

Dr. Creflo A.Dollar. Uprooting the Spirit of Fear. Tulsa Oklahoma: Harrison House 1994

Chuck D. Pierce, Rebecca Wagner Sytsema. When God Speaks. Colorado Springs, Colorado. Wagner Publications, 2003

Mary Geegh. God Guides. Wausau Wisconsin. Color Vision Printing Samuel and Lois Geegh and Marcy (Geegh) Zastrow, 2000

Leanne Payne. <u>Listening Prayer Learning to Hear God's Voice and Keep a Prayer Journal.</u> Grand Rapids Michigan. Baker Books 1994 and 2001

Cindy Jacobs. <u>The Voice Of God. How God Speaks Personally and Corporately to His Children Today.</u> Ventura California. Regal Books 1995

Joni Eareckson Tada. <u>The God I Love.</u> Grand Rapids, Michigan. Zondervan 2003

Steve Thompson. <u>You May All Prophesy.</u> North Carolina. Morningstar Publications 2003

Charles Stanley. <u>How to Listen to God.</u> Nashville, Atlanta, Camden, New York. Oliver Nelson 1985

James Wise. <u>Five Steps to Financial Freedom. Money Management Made Easy.</u> Tulsa Oklahoma. Hensley Publishing. 2003

Quinn Sherrer. <u>Listen, God is Speaking To You.</u> Ann Arbor, Michigan. Servant Publications – Vine Books. 1999

Printed in the United States
23255LVS00008B/298-399

9 781594 677748